ABOUT THE AUTHOR

Suhaiymah Manzoor-Khan is Muslim (someone who surrenders to the will of Allah), an educator, writer and spoken-word poet. She interrogates narratives around race/ism, Islamophobia, gender, feminism, state violence and decoloniality in Britain. She is the founder and author of the critical and educative blog, www.thebrownhijabi.com, and co-author of *A FLY Girl's Guide to University: Being a Woman of Colour at Cambridge and Other Institutions of Power and Elitism* (Verve, 2019). With a background studying History at Cambridge and Postcolonial Studies at SOAS, as well as a wider education from her mother and grandmother's wisdoms, the epistemology of Islam, and work of women of colour and anti-systemic thinkers from across the world, Suhaiymah's poetry is unapologetically political and deliberately unsettling. She isn't interested in your guesses or analyses.

Suhaiymah's poetry has over two million online views and since going viral as runner-up of the 2017 Roundhouse National Slam with her poem, *This Is Not a Humanising Poem*, she has performed on BBC Radio stations, at music festivals, in the US against Californian slam poets, across British Universities, on Sky TV, ITV, the Islam channel, Las Vegas, TEDxes, London poetry nights, mosques, protests outside the Home Office and in New York, Berlin, and Da Poetry Lounge in Los Angeles.

Postcolonial Banter is Suhaiymah's debut collection. It features some of her most well-known and widely performed poems as well as some never-seen-before material. Her words are a disruption of comfort, a call to action, a redistribution of knowledge and an outpouring of dissent. Whilst enraged and devastated by the world she finds herself in, in many ways it is also the mundane; hence, whilst political and complex in nature, her poetry is just the 'banter' of everyday life for her and others like her. Ranging from critiquing the function of the nation-state and rejecting secularist visions of identity, to reflecting on the difficulty of writing and penning responses to conversations she wishes she'd had; Suhaiymah's debut collection is ready and raring to enter the world.

Suhaiymah Manzoor-Khan
Postcolonial Banter

VERVE
POETRY PRESS
BIRMINGHAM

PUBLISHED BY VERVE POETRY PRESS
https://vervepoetrypress.com
mail@vervepoetrypress.com

FIRST PUBLISHED SEP 2019

Printed and bound in the UK
by TJInternational, Padstow

ISBN: 978-1-912565-24-5

NOTE FROM THE AUTHOR

بِسْمِ اللهِ الرَّحْمٰنِ الرَّحِيْمِ

Having spent the last eight years writing poems that were only
ever read and spoken aloud by me, writing a collection that
anybody can read as and where they want has been daunting.
With spoken-word poetry there is always the chance to explain
yourself, to clarify, to extend and contextualise to the audience
– with page poetry that feels less true and therefore, scarier.
However, to bridge the gap for myself I have included what I
am calling 'context boxes' throughout this collection. These
are boxes of information that explain some context about the
poem or background information I think is important. I want
the people I love and the people who these poems are for to
enjoy these poems, they're not just for self-proclaimed
readers, poets and artists, so I hope the boxes make this
collection more accessible; I'm not interested in writing poetry
for people to puzzle over or feel intimidated by – I'd rather
you puzzle over your reactions and responses. The boxes also
sometimes include recommended readings, or places to find
further information – please do use them as I'd like to think of
this collection as an educative toolkit of sorts.

Thank you.

CONTENTS

6

Acknowledgements

Postcolonial Banter

1

THIS POEM IS NOT FOR YOU

this poem is not for you

you can't wear it on your forehead
it won't look good in your profile picture
and I know you wish it was more colourful already
but I'm sorry
this poem is not for you

not like the last one
which wasn't for you either
but you told me was no good
told me to stop speaking it
told me you'd hurt me if I didn't

then took it behind my back, didn't you?
told your friends how *you* wrote it

well this poem is not for you,
I remembered not to write it down this time
though you're no novice to stealing thoughts themselves, remember?

that time you flashing-light siren whip-downed my door
cut out my tongue
and told me yours was better?
yeah
I never found where the old one went
so now my grandma can't always understand
and my God I wish I could write poems for her instead of you

my God
in a different language
mere Allah

do you remember the boys from school?
how you'd tell me their art was mud dark pretension way
below a C?
and the girls in the changing rooms?
you'd say poems are for the empty legs and tanned-not-brown
shoulder blades

well, this poem is not for you
and it isn't for your sister either actually
cos we're not
despite you telling me how similar we are
every time I see her
she looks straight through me

and my grandmother told me as well you know
how they used to laugh
your sisters with the now pierced noses
told her only animals do that

and she'll never forget that time you left us by the water's edge
her hands were full of it
and you said drink
work hard
goodbye
so we tried to
but my God the salt
and we only had our hands didn't we?
only had our hands

tell me, could you hear our shouts by then?
my mother was screaming "go back where you came from!"
but there was no re-wombing of the sea

so we're here now
where I'm telling you
this poem is not for you
but the number of times I've said it
makes me doubt it

and if it is for you
then at least let me tell you
don't you dare file it away some place
don't you dare blink-nod it into the "race" draw
or "mm"-scrunch-eye it into the "colonialism" cupboard
don't token-applaud it into the "feminism" lever-arch
I can see you doing it now

this poem is beyond you

it will never sit on your skin the way my colour sits on mine
you will never find it fallen down the floorboards after ten years
you will never study it at gcse
and most of all
you will never feel it pass between you and a stranger in a way
that says

I understand

I wrote this poem for the first heat of the Roundhouse Poetry Slam,
2017. It stemmed from my frustration with poetry slams themselves
because the last big slam (competition) I had been a part of made me
very aware that slam poets often perform our identities and trauma for
an audience to consume. To my mind this often means an
overemphasis on racial trauma for the sake of applause (and specifically
white audiences) and I felt frustrated thinking about how this
interaction reproduces many problematic dynamics of people of colour
'performing' for white voyeurism, approval and consumption. This
poem explores these feelings, drawing a parallel to the way so many
aspects of our identities are only approved/applauded once filtered
through whiteness or consumed by the white gaze.

WHERE IS MY HISTORY?

My history is imprinted in the spaces between the ink printed on
pressed pages
My history is the screams shouting out through the silent slots in
syllabi
it is caged in glass cases said to be for its own safety by the
institutions which narrate it as their own

because my history lies in the choices not recorded
about which stories should be hoarded
and called archives

and my archives
are the chicken shops
the taxi stops
the backseats of rentals
and inside hems of headscarves

women's conversations
women's congregations
women's contemplations

which you won't find in your local heritage site

No, cos my history is the shame of your history
the body buried in the back garden with no gravestone
but in fact not so shameful, no

For it is also adorning your proudest buildings
the ones I'm searched before entering
as if my bringing something in would be disturbing
as if my things weren't already coveted and stolen
sorry, read: salvaged and reallocated
to make up these museums in the first place

It's almost as if History is less about what happened
than maintaining ideology

'cos when you investigate a story
with half the participants absent
and don't worry about the translation
want only to fit the narrative to the nation
then is it surprising that what's surmised
is that my history is not?

That my past is 'culture' and 'ancient kingdoms'
never 'politics' or 'philosophy'

My ideas are 'religion' and 'oriental'
'tribes', 'norms', and alternative remedies
whilst yours are universal teleologies
and superior methodologies

No, it's no surprise my past is passed over
and pushed into the peripheries
despite being palpable in every premise of what gives Britain history

'cos to find it would be to remember
that if Britain is tudors and victorians
it's also Slavers and Plantations
the Colonies and the Colonised

To find my past would be to remember that
every object in the museum
that is said to be objectively seen
was plundered and stripped of value
for the perusal of researchers and big purses
to spectate and win awards

Whilst those of us who are still seen as 'backwards'
who don't get the time or space to explore artefacts
are in fact the outcome of their unnarrated relations
to colonial plunder and false salvation

So when you ask where my past is,
ask instead
what yours is without mine?

This poem was written as a commission piece for the launch of the
'Don't Settle' project looking at how local history is narrated with
young people in Birmingham, 2019. The main question of the launch
night was *where is my past?* which this poem was a response to. As a
History student with interest in thinking about what counts as history,
or as valuable knowledge, I loved writing this poem. The poem grap-
ples with the question of where my past is on three different levels.

On one level, 'where' my past is is a question of where it is in what is
called the subject of History. E.G. my past is missing from textbooks,
curriculums and documentary and other recordings of History in
the sense that if the history of e.g. Pakistan's creation is told, it is told
through the eyes of diplomats, South Asian elites and Britons with
their own assumptions and political goals. Or in the case of migration,
the history of Pakistani migrants to the UK is told as part of the history
of 'migration' which obscures the role of British colonialism and the
commonwealth in that migration. It also often obscures the place of
women – who are not only excluded from 'migrant' histories but also
'women's history' (for being migrants), and larger 'British history', too.
Such placement of my history is an outcome of the decisions that go
into selecting what is an historical document and what is not – e.g.
what piece of evidence is an important part of the story of 'The Past'
and what piece of evidence is not: what is a scribble on a piece of paper
and what is a 'source', what is an oral history and what is a story told by
a grandma? The decisions that make some sources/stories about the
past more 'valid' are not accidental but always political – the stories we
tell about the past are stories we are trying to consolidate about
the present. So, for example, if we suggest that 'the history of South

Asia' is a history mainly of colonisation and 'civilising', we privilege sources from diplomats and literate elites, but if we decide it is a history of e.g. rural women's everyday lives and subversion of oppressive external and internal forces, we would have to find a different way to think about sources and narratives – what don't they say? What is absent? Why?

On the second level, 'where' my past is is a question of artefacts and archives. It is well known that British colonial plundering means that places like 'the British Museum' are full of art, treasures and artefacts from around the world. Having them in that museum frames them as 'British' without placing them in the historical context of how they came to be in Britain – e.g. colonisation and conquest. In another context such objects would have a different narration and reveal a different history. Sources are never neutral and their meanings are never objective.

On the final level, 'where' my past is ideologically is that it is often placed outside of 'history' and instead into 'alternative' disciplines of 'religion' or 'non-European' history even though Europe makes no sense without 'global history'. Again, this is political. What we name things is an act of deciding what value they have and also a decision about whether or not we will face up to their present-day implications. If we say Britain's history is only that of Tudors and Victorians (devoid of the slavery and colonisation which was essential to those eras) then we suggest that there is absolutely no connection and thus no reason why people of colour are in Britain today – the context is erased and therefore present day exclusion is justified by historical exclusion.

Suggested reading:
Dipesh Chakrabarty, *Provincialising Europe: Postcolonial Thought and Historical Difference*, 2000.
Ramon Grosfoguel, '*Decolonising Post-colonial Studies and Paradigms of Political Economy*,' 2011.
Gyanendra Pandey, '*In Defense of the Fragment*', 1992.
Lola Olufemi, Odelia Younge, Waithera Sebatindira, Suhaiymah Manzoor-Khan, *A FLY GIRL'S GUIDE TO UNIVERSITY: Being a woman of colour at Cambridge and other institutions of power and elitism*, 2019.

PAKI

The first time my brother comes home from school
and uses the word Paki
I flinch. Gasp.
Almost spill the milk
I tell him *NO*
that is not a word we use to talk about ourselves

What I do not tell him
what hovers in the space between my words
is that that is a word only other people use about us
a word to crush and hurt us
a word to own us

but not be owned by us
The second time my brother comes home from school
and uses the word Paki
my mother admonishes him
tells him how that word was used to break her bones
when she was a child
tells him the neighbours would think he had
no respect for himself if they heard him

What hangs in the air, unspoken
is that that is because Paki deserves no respect
that to say it
might remind them
that our skins are not white
and to our ancestors
this was never home

My grandfather pores over a 3 inch
pixelated photograph on a phone-screen
cradled in his muscular autumnal hands

Hands that taught themselves
how cotton was spun in Bradford mills
where the lack of light
blurred young men's sight

Hands that held twenty-one grandchildren
in a foreign land
to give them hopes and dreams
on these streets paved with gold
and lined with blackened terraced housing

That's not how it looked when I lived there
the words fall from his mouth
fifty-five years heavy with the weight of not forgetting home

The third time my brother comes home from school
and uses the word Paki
I ask him why he is using it pejoratively
why he is synonymising it with Filth and Sub-par
he says that is the only way he has heard it being used before

So the fourth time my brother comes home from school
and uses the word Paki
I smile

I lead him to the kitchen
cut out our tongues
slice them up
and sew them back together in new shapes
relearning the language of our grandmother

I take him to the mirror
show him how to wipe
these ivory-white apologies
from our skin

I stand him in the garden
tell him to look up high
let the sun work her art on his beautiful face

We spit out sorry
and vomit attempts at assimilation
all over the grass
for assimilation without acceptance
is not that

The rain comes
and washes the dust
from our hands
a colour of pain

and this is what it is to be a Paki

This is one of my oldest poems. I wrote it after watching This Is
England '83. The film has a scene where a South Asian shopkeeper is
harassed and beaten up in a practice of 'Paki-bashing' which was
common in 1970s/80s England. Before this scene I had only heard
about Paki-bashing from my family and about the way the slur
had been used against my parents and grandparents growing up in
Bradford. On reflecting upon the violence of the word and the way it
stripped the humanity from people from or of South Asian heritage.
I wrote this poem pondering over the way the word is used today and
whether and what 'reclamation' can look like. Ultimately, the violence
of the word feels too present to me and to the inter-generational
memories of my family.

NANA

my grandfather has had an affinity for death all his life

death was not a shadow that hung over him
but the very light-source he was drawn to

my mother says he talked about dying since she was a child
it's almost as if Allah is holding out especially
or maybe my childhood prayers payed off
in the echo of Nana's voice saying one day he'd go 'upstairs'
I'd plead, Allah let him and my Nani live forever

Nana would probably curse that prayer
I imagine he has prayed for death all his life
not in a sad way, but valiantly

and yet death has been perhaps the only thing life let him hold close
tight onto
he left everything behind
split the world half in half
worked the factory night shift in Bradford mills where cotton was
spun and eyesight lost

he never saw his mother pass
couldn't afford to go

now he can
but he's never been back

fifty-five years of dark winters and cold summers

I marvel at him
wonder what fear prevents him going
how far inside himself he lives
how many traumas underpin his love of death

he is a tall man
but smallness lurks in his eyes nowadays
and sometimes when I hug his hard body
I wonder at what age brown men are allowed to cry

or is that why he's courting death?
perhaps there are no tears left for this life
where the only language he could ever speak heartbreak in
was silence

NANI

she smells like untouched snow
and morning mountain dew
her fingers peel potato skins
like unwrapping giggles from children's lips
she coaxes rice grains into scoops
and evaluates inexact measurements exactly

one end of her scarf teases at her lip corners
where secrets are buried
and not only anguish but bright-eyed girl-child love-laughter
spilling from every inch of translucent hand skin
love like lemons
never quite squeezed dry

soft soft soft stomach hands cheeks
occasional tears in an ostracised tongue
rocking back and forth on her prayer chair
fingers count beads
like knitting patterns long forgotten

arms always full
kameez always colourful
tossing rice into mouth
stroking slices out of an apple
labouring labouring labouring
selling secret gold
for secret home to escape in case when they send us back
the asians were in kenya eighty years she always says

she slips money into children's hands with a two-eyed wink
and she is fresh fresh freshly bathed
clean like rose water
knees like old age
but lips murmur over english words
learning learning learning

she gave and she gives

BRITISH-BORN

Paper says 'British-born'
like that's all it is
just an accident,
they rubbed out 'British-raised'
desperately trying to deflect

Erasing the context and connection
the fact this society made him,
this land, this place, our words, our harm

but he's British-born, not British
Brit-ish, never British.

They say the birth-place is somehow random
place his motives in a foreign land
must be the fact of his grandparents blood
must be the fact of his skin

What a welcome from the heart of the Empire
Raj of the Raj
a massive thumbs up from the hand that sliced us.

British-born, not British-made
foreign goods somewhere deep inside

I am British-born, British passport
but neon hijab and signposted skin
scanner goes off, obviously
a woman feels over me and looks straight through me

random swabs are made
I am unmade

passport says British
her eyes say 'British-born', only.

'British-born' is a term often used in British media to describe perpetrators of violence who are Muslim. It was used frequently to refer to the men behind the 7/7 attacks. I wrote about the term because I find it a very cleverly constructed word with a deliberate purpose. 'British-born' has its first usage in texts written in the 1960s due to attempts to distinguish first-generation immigrants in Britain from their children, however, the term itself meant those children, born in Britain, continued to be excluded from the idea of 'Britain' and 'the nation'. The national origins of their parents were seen as the more important factor determining the nature of these children. Britain was just - almost incidentally - the place of their birth.

The term 'British-born' in its current usage (mainly to talk about Muslims) is just as problematic as in the past. It works to place Muslims who perpetrate acts of violence outside of the imagined British nation. This means their violence does not have to be connected to Britain or the context they've lived in, grown up in and been surrounded by – that just becomes the location of their exit from the womb. Therefore those contexts don't need to be scrutinised or investigated as potentially connected to or in any way accountable for the violence they perpetrated. The term subsequently works to displace the context from the question of violence, but also to place people of colour and Muslims who it is generally applied to, as outsiders to the British nation. Our birthplace and surroundings are implied to have less impact on us than our inherited and seemingly 'irredeemable foreignness' (Cynthia Weber, 2016) which means that 'backwardness', 'violence' and all the colonial stereotypes associated with 'foreign' places, are attached to us and our bodies regardless of our location. We carry the otherness in us, and it is this that makes us only 'British-born', not 'British'.

The term 'British-born' is also an example of the way 'Britain' cannot define itself beyond whiteness. The exclusion of people of colour from the imagined boundary of who and what counts as 'Britain'/'British' is just more evidence that Britain and Britishness can only be imagined as white. Therefore, no matter how hard some people of colour/ Muslims try to prove their 'integration', or 'assimilation' and 'Britishness', their very colour becomes the barrier to their belonging. The case of Shamima Begum being stripped of her citizenship in 2019 is a perfect example of this. She could be stripped of her British citizenship despite having no other citizenship because the Home Secretary was 'satisfied' she could receive citizenship elsewhere. What made him assured of this? Simply put, her colour – the Otherness within her - due to her colour it was assumed there was another place that she could belong to/really came from. Ironically this presumption was completely flawed and the Bangladeshi government refused to give Shamima citizenship. This example illustrates the power of imagining the nation, the importance it has for excluding certain populations, and the practical implications of such ideological boundary making.

A PRAYER FOR THOSE WHO JEER AT THE DEATH OF A BABY WHOSE TEENAGE MOTHER YOU FEEL DID NOT SHOW ENOUGH REMORSE

May you never feel the weight of what makes you human stripped from your bones.

May you never know malnutrition or untimely death.

May you always be warm.

May you never see enough war that a bodiless head does not disturb you.

May you never be alone and vulnerable.

May your children not be preyed on.

May they never live in a place that tries to vomit them out.

May they never lose hope.

May safety cloak your shoulders when you stand to pray.

May you pray.

May you never know the heavy feeling of soil packed between your limbs whilst you're still alive.

May you never be a test for the oppressors.

May you never be unloved.

May people never feel satisfied that the treatment you get is the treatment you deserve.

May they give you a name when you die.

May they remember you as human.

May your death be mourned in fullness and not just a symbol in a bigger debate.

May you feel joy like the denseness of the night.

May it drown you like the mediterranean sea.

May it hit you in waves when you least expect it

crash through your door like bulldozers

occupy your home

smatter through your windows

spray you like bullets with your name on them

may you make a home in it

may you choke on it

breathe it

live it

die it

and may no one ever think they have a right to remove you from it.

2

A STORY FOR OURSELVES
THIS TIME

I do not know how to write us outside of bangles and anklets
gold and pretty
but still a type of chain.

I do not know how to write us outside of romance and tragedy
tears of joy or tears of grief
which for us too often are made the same.

I do not know how to write us outside of long hair and long eyelashes
which apparently suit us better than long lives.

I do not know how to write us outside of fear, yet
whispers and elisions and repeated mistakes
I wonder if our mothers promised they would not do the same.

I do not know how to write us outside of our mothers.
How not to make reference to their spines and silences
how to do it as more than a prelude to my own.

I do not know how to write us outside of men
their eyes, their grips, their words, their pleasure

I do not know how to see our bodies outside their hands
how to salvage our skin from their requirements
how to write us with hairy arms and upper lips
bushy eyebrows before they were fashionable
cracked heels, full bellies, and laughing mouths
not just kissing lips.

I want to know how to write us outside the kitchen
too often we are made into jasmine, cinnamon, and sugar
but we are onions, garlic, ginger
roots, tough, essential - the basis of everything, indispensable.

Too often we are made into the moon
a mere mimicry of another's light
but we are the sun, the blaze, the fiery depth
we are deadly and uncontainable.

Take back your rivers, your stars, your flowers
we are the source, the light, the soil.

I want to write us outside of beauty and myth, though
outside secrecy, shame, and marriage
outside of songs
outside of heartache
outside of staring eyes and lowered gaze.

I want to write us
even if I do not know how to begin
because at least that way
we'll be a story for ourselves this time.

I wrote this poem when I spent three months in Pakistan in 2018. I
kept trying to write a poem about the women I was surrounded by
but found that every time I tried, I would fall into stereotypes,
clichés and tropes of South Asian women. As I often do when I find
this happening, instead, I wrote a poem about the difficulty of writing
that poem.

VOICES ROLL OVER THE CHARPAI
for Allajaway

The only people I want to fall in love with me
are old women
not the kind that say I should wear more dresses
but the kind with cracked fingertips and black heels
the kind who can crouch between their legs and be at home

> Her naked calves in my naked hands
> she looks to the window and says
> *tannu milkar sanu barri khushee hoi*

The shy offering urges me to take the plunge
and the plunge feels more like floating
so I reach into it
squeezing the flesh of her right lower leg
I say, *mei aap ko boht pyaar karti hu*
adamantly focusing my eyes on her shin

> After nothing
> she says,
> *mei bee tannu barri pyaar karti*
> like an exhale
> her words clasp mine
> in a way that makes the walls sigh
> *at last*

I keep kneading below her knees
feeling both our lungs lighten
time sits up straight
every bird cranes ears through the window
the smell of coconut oil on my hands cocoons us
and the room is full of silence by a more delicate name

I do not need the love of anyone but old women
want only the secret glances and two-eyed winks of old women
only ache for the touch of hands with translucent skin
want only their laughter and half-toothed smiles

In the morning Nani revels in the sounds of the streets
reminds me that in England there is no *ronak* like this
no ronak like crushing peanuts in your palms by the roadside
no ronak like the type that emanates from her jawline
I remind her that in England there is no sitting like this either
with traffic washing over you like lullabies
with onions and sun cream engrained in your fingers

I do not need the love of anyone but old women
want only their affirmations and to bask in their brown
want only their strange remedies and fond shrugging nods

Voices roll over the charpai
like brown hands making roti

I understand like traces
and if I close my eyes I see orange

three echoes of brown feet crouch in the weaves
we are the sunlight on the roof

birds circle making handi of the sky
and laughter washes over us like wudhu

I do not need the love of anyone but old women
want only *their* eyes on me when I kick my legs up to the sky
want only *their* eyes on me as the adhaan dances through pink
edges of the air

when I leave I cry all the way home
I cry in the silence of a taxi ride
our six legs pressed together for a last time
I cry in the darkness of the plane
sat between two old women who aren't them

I watch her embrace me a thousand times
the flight of her kiss on my head never quite the same
I feel the tears rise again
we stand apart in silence again
she wipes her eyes with her shawl again
and we drive to the airport in silence again

sunlight shakes my hand through the plane window for a last time

aaja shaam honi ayee

I cry into my diary for a last time

mausum ne le ungrai

something about me is smaller

tho kis baath kee hai larayee

a piece left behind

tu chal

a breaking heart is a beautiful price to pay though

mei ayee

to get to leave a piece behind

chal, mei ayee

the only people I want to fall in love with me
are old women

بیچارے

he asks me if I know what this word means
becharay
he says we are

and by we he means two adult-children with brown bodies not meant
for cloudy islands
by we he means the accident of forgetting to go home
thinking you had one
staying too many nights, out too late
losing sight of where from was

becharay
he says it the way you console a grieving mother
who lost something she can't remember
to men who hailed from rainy places
and took her sun

he says it the way you kiss a forehead out of pity
like his lips are neither healing nor empty

becharay
I wonder if we are

Google says *be* meaning without
            chara meaning option/choice/alternative
I think about the choices I never made to be here
and other people's bending knees

I think about spaces that swallow you and vomit you at the same time
racist graffiti that appears overnight
bans that say you are not welcome in the place you never chose to
come but need to stay

becharay
he says it with a golden-blue smile
and later I tell him he has the archetypal terrorist look
and that sometimes I can't breathe because people think they already
know me

I think about how the shower water licks my shoulders like flames
and that the idea of drowning whilst burning is somehow too real

so when he asks me if I know what this word means
becharay
I say no
just to hear him say it
hear him tell me that we are

THE BREAKING BRANCH

he's falling on the breaking branch again
or more accurately
he's breaking on the falling branch

and I can't stop it

it isn't slow motion like how they say
it's over in a second
he's fallen he's broken I'm shaken
I'm holding the branch beneath me hard

but he was broken long before the branch
some lives just become their own metaphors
to gain the relief of an outsider's perspective

here I am
outsider
not knowing how to write him as more than a metaphor
how to write him without reducing him to the finger clicks
that will surely be scattered over his crumbling

because his crumbling is known to us
it's a familiar debris we know to hate but not much what else to do
it's the crumbling of mortgages that sap your sleep before your pocket
the crumbling of arms that punch much better than they hold
the crumbling of becoming what you hate because it's the only option

it's the crumbling white boys with beards and berets glorify
it's also probably where they get their supply

but they're not breaking on the falling branch
he is
and I don't know if you've ever tried to fix a branch back to a tree

it's not that it's not easy
it's not possible

DEATH WAS SMALLER THAN I ANTICIPATED

Death was smaller than I anticipated
no spotlight or looming shadow
just a blinking phone screen I could easily have missed

it seemed strange
although, I suppose
not as strange as you and I were to each other

I potted my avocado sap at last
had been meaning to for months
but after I received the text
I thought something about the cycles of life
and it felt right to smell soil about now

Later I caught myself laughing in the shower
distracted and amused
I abruptly stopped and frowned in the mirror

it seemed inappropriate
although, I suppose
not as inappropriate as you and I not knowing each other

If death is just another facet of distance
I am less sad that you are gone
than that the possibility of restoration between us is

For someone who clutches my history like a lifeline
and sings of women whose pasts are extensions of my own
it is strange I carried on eating my porridge

I will always be a half-true narrative to myself now
with you go all archives of my past
the full context of my being here

I hope Allah forgives me
and you
for eating chunks out of each others' books
parallel universes where grandmothers and grandchildren
hold hands

I don't even know if your skin was translucent
in that way old womens' go
I don't even know if our hands were the same size

It seems silly to write for you now you're not here to read it
although, I suppose
not as silly as not knowing you at all

3

ISLAMOPHOBIA 101

[commission for MEND for Islamophobia Awareness Month 2018]

The mother and her children getting spat at in the street
The student whose home is raided over a word googled for a
worksheet

The man interrogated at the airport because of how he looks
The pressure on the employee to not kick up a fuss

The frowning face that tells you, you deserve to be harassed
The dreadful silence on the bus of people looking past

This is Islamophobia
it's not accidental, random, or irrational
it's every day, everywhere
a problem that's international

The woman making herself small in the corner of her train seat
The children whose school went from 'Outstanding' to 'Special
Measures' in a heartbeat

The difference in numbers of memorials when Muslim lives are lost
The well-founded concerns that our phone-calls and homes are being
watched

The contradictory calls to 'go back where you came from' *and*
assimilate
The negative stereotyping of us as suspects that they like to perpetuate

This is Islamophobia
it's not just personal and prejudicial
it's complicated, historical
and very deeply structural

The condemnation of Islam as a threat to freedom of speech contrasted with
The legal requirement on teachers to monitor the Muslim students that they teach

The demonization of a demographic made to face constant scrutiny
The group of men scapegoated so we ignore broader issues of foreign policy and misogyny

The irony that 'protecting democracy' means Muslim's democratic rights are breached
The secret courts, deportations, inhumane arms deals, and yet no one impeached

This is Islamophobia
it's not accidental, random, or irrational
it's monetised, ideological
and treats all Muslims as criminal

The unironic accusation of 'intolerance' whilst refusing to tolerate us at all
The pressure to fit shifting boxes and prove 'moderation' or be labelled 'radical'

The assumption that violence is caused by a 'Muslim mentality'
The way this allows society to ignore broader questions of governmentality

The powerful figures spreading hatred that depends on lies and myths
The refusal of those around them to see it, their pretending it doesn't exist

This is Islamophobia
it's not just personal and prejudicial
it's no accident, or random fear
it's been cultivated to be here

Have you seen it
in the comments, the headlines, and the tweets?
Have you heard it
in the office, the classrooms and the streets?

Did you stop it?
Will you next time?
Can you see the larger view?

After all, as the old saying goes
if you don't stand up for us,
what's to stop them coming for you?

WE DID NOT BRING THIS DARKNESS UPON OURSELVES

it is an ordinary week day
or as ordinary as they come nowadays
which is to say
there is a car parked in the back street

parked a little too long
so my mother heads outside

two men sit dawdling

she asks what they're here for
they say *we're fixing the water*

but because my mother is an immigrant woman
she knows you don't take white men at their word

especially not ones in uniform

so later
when a different man comes in a different van
and climbs the telephone pole outside her window
she watches on

and later
when she laughs with unsmiling eyes and says
he installed a black box on the telephone pole
- it's directly facing the bathroom window

we roll our eyes

as if to both acknowledge what she did not say
and to suppress it
but because our mother is our mother
we know that suppressing her fear will not suppress our own

so although we laugh when she tells us
every day after that no one mentions that we keep the bathroom
light off at night

I wonder if we brought this darkness upon ourselves

I wonder if other people live like this

I know instinctively that they do not

I know instinctively that I should laugh

but we grew up surrounded by unfunny jokes

with friends who told us to turn phones off when they came around
with biro pens at the ready to write location names down
with an unacknowledged agreement
that the kitchen wall may be tapped
pressing the soft belly of a squeaky toy puppy when we wanted to
say certain words

I know instinctively that I shouldn't tell anyone that
that if I did they'd think we're crazy

that it is crazy

that we are

because we are

We're All Crazy Here

and by crazy I mean our reality is Not Believable To The Listener

by crazy I mean in a state of constant hypervigilance
by crazy I mean constant hypervigilance is the first symptom of
trauma
and I mean that targeted racism is trauma on a mass scale
being made helpless again and again every day repeat, repress,
replay
standing stock still
adrenaline pumping
no means to fight
nowhere to flight
fearing the repetition
it coming anyway

by crazy I mean wearing the stories of others around our necks

by crazy I mean there is nothing left to trust

by crazy I mean seeing ourselves targeted every day

by crazy I mean in pain

I mean devastated anxious unable to sleep
slumped shoulders and aching backs

by crazy I mean that if you believe me then you're crazy too
because crazy is a reality not believable to the listener

but because I am a woman, grown
I know that being crazy is not the worst thing you can be

ducking to wash your hands is not the worst way to live

using the bathroom in the dark is not the strangest thing
people have done

we did not bring this darkness upon ourselves

and even if and when a black box is just a black box
we know black boxes that weren't

do you not remember that time his house was raided?
do you not remember The Girl Kicked Down The Stairs?
Do You Not Remember The Home Office Funded CCTV?
Do You Not Remember The 'Secret' Evidence Used To Extradite?

Do You Not Remember They Don't Want Us Here?

Do You Not Remember We Are Suspect?

Do You Not Remember They Want Us To Build Prisons Out Of Our
Communities?

To Build Prison Guards Out Of Ourselves?

That We Are Both Captives And Nearly-Caught?

Both Dangerous And Endangered?

Do You Not Remember Who We Are?

I know instinctively that I would rather duck
know instinctively that I should be embarrassed to say that
and know instinctively that I don't

for as long as I am in this body at this time, though I do not
know a lot
I know not to trust
I know that this is a police state
I know that I am unwanted
and I know no matter what I say what this still looks like

I Know That It Is Not Believable to The Listener

but I also know who I am
and I know that my history is a record of unbelievable things
that also

all

just happen to be true

I wrote this poem just after starting to read *The Body Keeps The Score* by Bessel van der Kolk. I read it because I'd seen it recommended multiple times as a key text to read if you want to understand trauma. The book explains how traumatic moments and the resulting stress have a physiological impact on our bodies and brains that have consequences for how we act, interact and experience our lives. In reading the book I became aware of how present trauma and its symptoms were and are in most of the people I most love and how so often the quirks of personalities which have become almost jokes amongst us about how paranoid, panicked or over-reacting we are – are all typical signs of someone who has experienced trauma. Reflecting on the normalisation of the feeling of unsafety in and amongst most people I love and am close to made me reflect on the traumas that they and we all experience. Alongside personal and interpersonal traumas was the obvious theme of racism. This poem came about as a reflection on the way racism and Islamophobia are intergenerational and communal experiences of trauma which sit in all our bodies and impact the ways that even those of us who have not directly experienced 'an attack', or 'a raid' or 'an interrogation' or 'entrapment' or 'being spied on' or 'being harassed', still carry the symptoms of those traumas such as hypervigilance and avoidance – this shows that the very nature of those violences are structural and systemic. I use the word 'crazy' in the poem deliberately - to comment on the way that the traumas we experience and their resulting effect on our mental health is completely stigmatised so that we (particularly women of colour) are portrayed to be illogical, ill and hysterical, rather than responding to the conditions of violence we live in.

RECIPE FOR A WAR ON TERROR

Note: Whilst there are many steps to this recipe you really need
only one ingredient: terror.
The problem is that this ingredient cannot be found naturally so
you will have to make it first, to go to war with it.

Step 1.

Equip, fund, and train men you simultaneously vilify, scapegoat,
and Other and have for centuries,
use them to fight proxy wars for you but keep this step of the recipe
as quiet as possible - these will be your future terrorists,
leave to simmer.

Step 2.

Whilst step 1 prepares itself build up some other reasons for war
not real reasons,
don't give away your priorities of course, just covers.

An example you might use is suggesting your involvement is
intervention
necessary to bring about peace and stop violations of human rights
and territorial integrity
*violations you turn a blind eye to when they aid your geopolitical
goals.

Hopefully no one will question this logic.[1]

---

[1] When Iraq violated Iran's territorial integrity in the 1980s this was not
deemed a violation as it aided the USA's geopolitical goals in the area
(particularly curbing the power of Iran after the Iranian revolution),
however, when it came to Iraq invading Kuwait in the 1990s it was deemed a
violation and led to US-led military assault (it now suited the USA's
geopolitical goals in the area).

Step 3.

Now that you have created belief in backwards, violent, foreign Others that you must go to war with in order to save from themselves it's time to go in.

Use words like *freedom* and *liberty* to make the blow seem less hard,

hopefully the men you trained and set aside in step 1 will now become appalled by your foreign policy and violent hypocrisy and will respond with violence of their own.

Step 4.

Jump on this violence.
If and when it happens go full throttle
make sure you use every means possible to call and determine that their violence is *terrorism,*
make sure you use every means possible to call and determine that your *own* violence is *not terrorism,*
this is central to make the oxymoron, War On Terror, ignorable.

Some ways you might distance your violence from terrorism include:

1. Trying the line that women abroad are oppressed by foreign men and that bombs and war are the only way to liberate them.
Hopefully no one will question this logic.

2. You might suggest that foreign lands suffer from lack of freedom and democracy and that only bombs and war can bring about due civic process.
Perhaps even name your invasion: "Operation Enduring Freedom".[2]
Hopefully no one will question this logic.

---

[2] The official name used by the Bush administration to refer to their invasion of Afghanistan.

Step 5.

Now that you are at war abroad there may be some opposition at home, it is important to dehumanise those you are at war with enough that people at home stop caring whilst you extend the war-front.

A quick way to dehumanise those you are at war with is to suggest they are utterly and completely different from you and that they are threats to you.

An example you might use is suggesting that foreign countries are hiding weapons and men who want to harm your country,
this creation of mass panic and terror is essential to justify your own war *on* terror.

Hopefully no one will question this logic.

Note: this step will have negative consequences for those who look like the ones you are at war with in your own country, but don't worry, whilst this may seem a negative side-effect it will in fact be quite useful in the long run.

For example:

Step 6.

If opposition at home really starts brewing it will only worsen things to respond with explicit coercion.

Instead, bring in authoritarian measures through a more subtle route by actually reinforcing the idea that those who look like the ones you are at war with in your own country
are potential threats.

Based on the dehumanisation you've been involved in since step 1 and the illegitimate reasons for war since step 2 it is in fact possible that some of those who look like the ones you are at war with in your own country might respond to violence with violence,

if and when they do – again - jump on it.

Introduce mass surveillance, secret courts, swifter deportation measures, border stops and increased policing.

Bring these things in through the guise of safeguarding and preventing terrorism

suggest that voicing opinions against the war may be a sign of radicalisation

this will also help deflect the original grievances against your war – double whammy!

Step 7.

Don't go too far though.
Make sure it doesn't seem that you actually want and need to Other those who look like the ones you are at war with in your own country.

Say aloud *Islam is a religion of peace*
you don't think all Muslims are terrorists, only a minority
- that phrasing is key - really hammer it home
it still allows you to make *all* Muslims scapegoats and suspects since how else could you find out which are part of the "minority"?

Step 8.

Not crucial but helpful:
whilst you dehumanise, scapegoat violence, and deflect dissent you can also gain more support at home and tighten control of society by deflecting any other grievances onto these foreign Others too.

Some examples you might use include:
1- Suggesting the foreign Others all hate women,
this will help cover up the violent misogyny of your own society.
Hopefully no one will question this logic.

2- Suggesting the foreign Others are all inherently homophobic.
This will help cover up your own murderous treatment of queer
people at home.

Note: to prevent any potential questioning of this make a show of
equal marriage and a woman Prime Minister but keep killing poor,
non-white, and immigrant women and queers.

Hopefully no one will question this logic.

Step 9.

Whilst your war has been bubbling away there may have been some
problems in the background but don't worry, even if you run out of
initial reasons for war you've now made yourself a new and endless
enemy to be at war with:
Muslims in general.

*but remember, only a minority
** but remember, that could be any of them

Subtly suggest that Muslimmness itself is criminal
make wearing hijab, praying, being bearded or of darker complexion
reasons for suspicion,
tell schools, universities and hospitals to look out for these signs
make them punishable offenses worthy of stop and search, detention,
even citizenship deprivation.

You can now round-up, arrest or even exile dissenters without
reasonable justification - you have an enemy for the war *and* a reason
to clamp down on protest!

Step 10.

Torture or entrap the people you detain until they give false evidence
to admit some terror related crimes,[3]
you do need to keep the image going after all,
especially because people might start asking questions when refugees
begin flooding your borders.

*the long term consequences of steps 1-3
**sorry, we forgot to mention that at the start

At this point we advise you to simply repeat steps 6-10 as many times
as you need, adjusting to the context appropriately.

You have terrorised the world with your War on Terror after all
so violence is likely to continue
even as you assert your desire to stop it by engaging in it.

Hopefully, no one will question this logic.

---

[3]see Arun Kundnani, *The Muslims Are Coming: Islamophobia, Extremism and the
Domestic War on Terror*, 2014, or watch some interviews with him on Youtube to
understand his argument.

When I first began to research the history and roots of 'The War on Terror' and connect it to the current situation of Muslims in Britain I felt that there was such a formulaic and almost logical cause-and-effect sequence of events that made the past 30 or more years comprehensible that it was absurd. Placed in historical context the entire 'War on Terror' had an obvious political function and it worked to disguise, displace and hide so many power dynamics and political decisions that it was farcical. This 'recipe' poem therefore came out of reflecting on the political motives and reasons for the 'War on Terror', as opposed to the rhetoric given and displayed around it.

The poem's steps broadly follow a chronology of events from the 1980s, with step 1 referring to the fact that the USA and other governments supported, trained, financed and equipped Afghan mujahideen guerrilla fighters against the Soviets during the Soviet-Afghan War 1979-1989 and that the origins of al-Qaeda can be traced to these guerrilla groups and fighters who the CIA funnelled hundreds of millions of dollars into throughout the 1980s. The steps go on to reference the Gulf Wars and US interest in 'the middle east', 9/11 as a precursor to the invasion of Afghanistan and then to war in Iraq and the simultaneous building of Counter Terror apparatus domestically in the UK and USA. I try to follow the way that the logics of the Counter Terror apparatus relied on and came out of the fear-mongering around terrorism and associating it with any/all Muslims. As Arun Kundnani writes, 'Islamophobia is a form of structural racism directed at Muslims and the ways in which it is sustained [is] through a symbiotic relationship with the official thinking and practices of the war on terror'. And as David Harvey writes, 'It was the war on terror, swiftly followed by the prospect of war with Iraq, which allowed the state to accumulate more power.'

Finally, I want to quote at length from Richard Jackson on the way that the language of the 'War on Terror' works. He said, even in 2005, 'it is a deliberately and meticulously composed set of words, assumptions, metaphors, grammatical forms, myths and forms of knowledge – it is a carefully constructed discourse - that is designed to achieve a number of key political goals: to normalise and legitimise the current counter-terrorist approach; to empower the authorities and shield them from criticism; to discipline domestic society by marginalising dissent or protest; and to enforce national unity by reifying a narrow conception of national identity. The discourse of the 'war on terrorism' has a clear *political* purpose; it works for someone and for something; it is an exercise of power'.

Further reading:

Arun Kundnani, *The Muslims are Coming: Islamophobia, Extremism, and the Domestic War on Terror.* 2014.

Richard Jackson, *Writing the War on Terrorism, Language, Politics and Counter-Terrorism,* 2005.

David Harvey, *The New Imperialism,* 2003.

THE BEST OF THE MUSLIMS

The Good Muslim is a compliant subject
stating no subjectivity
making no demands for state accountability
merely proving peacefulness and accommodating hostility

The Good Muslim is a silent Muslim
who worships, foremostly, acceptability

The Bad Muslims are the Extremists
the Distorters
and the Radicals

they're told,
Come Back to The Middle
Be Balanced
Be Moderate

Without consideration that what's central
is circumstantial
and we must scrutinise the context before claiming it's correct.

After all is it not suspicious that Moderate
aligns so closely with Liberal Values?
And Holding Liberal Values
happens to denote Obedient Citizenship?
And Obedient Citizenship means 'be blind to colonialism'
'don't complain about the racism'
'neoliberalise your identity so modest fashion is enough'
'integrate or deserve deportation'
'at the same time tolerate dehumanisation'
'and know that anyway, we'll never accept you as having fit in'

Is it not suspicious that Moderate Muslim
fits so easily into Western analytical categories?
Ones which came into existence a millennia after the Quran?
It's almost as if Moderation has less to do with theology
than hegemony

and more to do with worshiping the nation-state
than submission of the soul

I'd rather be a Bad Muslim than a Good Muslim
because such labels don't signify piety
they just distance us from the reality
masquerading as statuses with neutrality
bounding us and binding us
leaving us defined by external demand

So now the only Good Muslim is a silent Muslim
The Good Muslim is an excuse to condemn the rest
and all that really means is that in their eyes
if you want to be of those who pass the test
the Best of all the Muslims
                                    is a Muslim who's not

Recommended reading:
Farid Esack, 2013, 'Redeeming Islam: Constructing the Good Muslim Subject in the Contemporary Study of Religion', *Alternation Journal*, 11, 36-60.

Upon reading this article I felt moved to write this poem. It was one of the strongest articulations of the creation of the 'Good Muslim' vs 'Bad Muslim' dichotomy that others have often written about; see, Mahmood Mamdani, *Good Muslim Bad Muslim: America, The Cold War, and the Roots of Terror* (2004). I strongly reject the idea of 'good' ('secular', 'western') and 'bad' ('extreme', 'traditional') Muslims because the very dichotomy and associated categories have no inherent meaning or connection to Islam, they purely serve a political function that works to regulate Muslim people's behaviours and keep us always in the position of 'proving' our 'goodness'. In my opinion this is a complete distraction from the work that needs to be done, and moreover, it can never be done because the tragic catch-22 of the construct is that no matter how 'good' one proves oneself to be, their 'Muslimness' itself will always jeopardise and put that 'goodness' into scrutiny and disbelief.

4

EXISTING IN BIG WAYS

1.
what would being safe look like?
what would it look like to feel truly safe?
how would that sit on our bodies?

would it look like being free to walk aimlessly in the night?
would it look like being free to walk aimlessly in the day?
would it look like sitting with legs spread wide open on a train?

what would it feel like to be so big we were safe?
what would it feel like to be dark and big and safe?
to exist in *big* ways
to take up space

to be big beyond the names men leave us with
big enough that white people don't shatter those names in their
mouths

to be big beyond borders
to be spilling over seas over lands over seas
too big for prisons
too big for detention centres
so big that bullets bounce off
so big they can't deport us
too big for natural disasters
tornadoes and tsunamis

big like superpowers
big like blocking bulldozers that come to smash your door down
big like keeping the door closed to riot police
big like small children's dreams

big enough to turn the earth's orbit in another direction
big enough to move mountain ranges back under the sea
so big no one steals the land from us the first time
so big we don't think of the land as ours

so big that we are the land
all the land is us
and there is no land or us there is you and me and we and we and we
so big that I am you
that I can't hurt you 'cos your pain is my pain

so big we belong
so big we *are* belonging
so big they can't reduce us to here or there or in-between

so big we don't drown this time

so big we're stationary

so big they can't kick us out
there is no in or out there is only round and round and round
so big we're a universe
so big we matter

so big that when we cry the world ends

so big that when we cry the world ends

2.
but what about being too big?
big like the only way I know you're big is that there's someone left
small
big like making someone else feel small

big like unfair
like overexpansion
like *that's actually someone else's space*

big like empire
like colonisation
like danger

like a blooming flower that is not a flower but a tree
not a tree but a forest
not a forest but a forest fire
big like a forest fire burning down a mountain side

big like mountains crumbling to dust
like yawm-al-qiyammah
like destruction

like *he can't breathe, stop, he can't breathe, can't you see he can't breathe -*

big like big boys
big boys don't cry
big boys hurt and hurt and hurt

big like violence
not the word but the thing it describes
not the time it takes for the bullet to leave his gun and hit your neck
but big like the time that time takes to process

big like grief
like genocide
like speaking over us
like erasing us
like no one is listening
like you may as well be background noise

3.
why are we afraid to be small though?
we want to be so big so big so big so big so big
why are we afraid to be insignificant?
afraid to be inconsequential?
to be so small we go unseen
to be so small we rely on one another
so small that alone we are nothing

why are we afraid to be nothing?

JUST A JULY

it was Sunday again
and then it was Sunday again
it was Sunday again and again

I was always brushing my teeth in the mirror
one perpetual opening credits I couldn't play past

the weeks must have fallen
between the floorboards
or got mixed in with the old bus tickets in my coat pocket

either way I was living in an autumn
though it was the hottest July on record

a July of perpetual Sundays
and brushing my teeth in the mirror

and there was that one night the moon turned red
and there was that storm the nation had waited for
but I missed both
probably brushing my teeth in the mirror

I didn't *lose* any friends
but they were those bus tickets
around somewhere
unnecessary, to be thought about later

even so
I was lonely
not in that gut-wrenching way
not like someone lobbed an arm off
but more like after a haircut
that feeling that something's just off

I didn't mind
or wouldn't have if I'd walked more
and I convinced myself that if I just had a new bike
I'd be content

not that I wasn't

not that I wasn't

just

I was autumning
and we don't have cocoons or caves for that like other animals
we just have cages
and prison boxes
to seek and await the change in

I was afraid of growing older
or no
afraid of doing it wrong

I googled my name some mornings
just to reassure myself I had been somewhat worthwhile

did I think about death?
yes
not in a bad way
just like when you prepare for a holiday a few months away
it crossed my mind
probably when I brushed my teeth in the mirror
and I'd have morbid urges to archive my life

half my room was perfect
cleared out
minimal
the other half was full of boxes

I slept in the middle
always soundly
but never long enough

I was okay though
just needed to shower a bit more
I would be okay
I'd look back on this as just a July

A POEM THAT WINDS THROUGH LEWISHAM STREETS

on Ramadan nights I feel like a poem
a poem that winds through Lewisham streets
a poem that is a girl
girl in trackies and abaya
socks in sandals hitting pedals

bike wheels a rhythm to her dhikr
shadow bops one-two one-two whilst passing street lights
one-two one-two subhanallahi wa bihamdihi

moon shines brighter on Ramadan nights
so does girl's heart

girl feels like a poem striding into a mosque
unfurls abaya in same motion as locking bike

people look
or maybe no one looks
girl can't say because girl doesn't look

girl walks into mosque
mosque is a poem
sensory overload
smells like skin smells like shoes smells like women
women's skin women's shoes

mosque is a girl in a mosque
head rounded dome-like gazing downwards
legs rooted firmly to the ground side by side
cacophony of nations
voices like hands sliding over each other in *salaam*

girl thinks of writing a poem when praying
thinks praying is a poem - no incentive but another world

Allah wrote poems
girl is one of Allah's poems
mosque is one of Allah's poem
girl is a poem inside mosque poem inside world poem

forehead to ground
side by side
Allah makes girl a metaphor for submission
surrender, humility

Allah makes girl a simile to herself
a reminder of her final destination

girl shuffles out of mosque
one of so many
no one seeing her / Allah seeing her

girl notes to self to write a poem
a poem that can wind through Lewisham streets
a poem about the girl poem Allah already wrote
about how that poem never feels more alive
than soaring downhill, scarf in wind
on the way back from mosque on Ramadan nights

FOR 2006

how are you?
the words tumble from me
so familiar
and he too
even here
in this twenty-something precipice

we're six
and it's sports day
and we're both Green Team

we're eight
and he tags me
every time in bulldog

it's not like being on the clever table anymore
he says

in those words
and his puckered up eyes
I taste the sour milk
of childhood long gone

he shakes my hand
and I can barely hear him
just feel the rough
rough boy hands

he says he reads Chinese philosophy
because he's bored
and his memory is not so good anymore

the memory of smoke
caresses his cheeks
and for a moment
I see the ten year old he says he hopes I will remember him as

regret stains his lips
and I remember
at ten we both wore shorts to school
and he told me to make sure they play *hoppipolla* at his funeral

that memory catches in my throat
and in his sincere eye-contact
so I tell him and he smiles
the first real smile
like seeing someone who loves you
when you're far from home

here we are ten minutes from our childhood homes
and ten years too far
for him

ten years or more too far from the clever table
and childhood shorts

he sports a coat that would hide your secrets
and eyes that are ashamed
because they let me stay at the clever table
someone approved me and not him

he asks, *what is clever, anyway?*
and we're five years old
sipping milk from the glass bottle
and we both are

clever

Theatres

act i scene i
small brown girl stands in a red jaw full of white teeth
tier upon tier
she appears uncomfortable, alone
dressed her best but not good enough

small brown girl sits facing the Stage Direction
laughs when others laugh
makes sure not to whisper *too loud*
slips secret maltesers out of her bag
slips secret maltesers into her mouth
makes sure not to rustle *too loud*
pretends she is not affronted by the price of ice cream
pretends this is not a birthday gift but an everyday expense

pretends

small brown girl sinks into the dimming lights
her act is almost over now

'cos going to the theatre is the performance they don't review
there is no play so scrutinised as us
no costume designer so determined to get it right
look the part
say *we belong here too*

if a theatre is not a nation
why does the threshold feel like a border?
why are there border police?
why does going in make you feel like you could be kicked out?

act i scene ii
small brown girl's mother ranked theatre up with private schools
and piano lessons
childhoods that could trick them into treating you better
could curtain-call you into respectability

so small brown girl attended ballet classes but never made the cut
small brown girl looked at listings where roles for small brown girls
never showed up
small brown girl spent weeks learning the steps to Hairspray for the
school production
but it was in the title
                        *hair*spray
                                    they said it just wouldn't add up

act ii scene i
big white man asks small brown girl
are you in the right place?
are you lost?
the cinema is two streets away

big white man does not say aloud but asks small brown girl anyway
how could you afford this?
how could you be this?
you are an imposter.

act ii scene ii
white woman asks small brown girl
advise me on a play I'm writing
it's about a muslim girl facing an identity crisis
what do you think?

small brown girl thinks white woman should write about something
she knows about

small brown girl thinks white woman's muslim girl makes no sense
how is she on the stage when she can barely sit in the audience yet?

but then again theatres are full of applause that doesn't add up
stories that say they are for one person but packaged for another

they would rather standing ovation a version of me written by
someone else
than share my armrest

act ii scene iii, final scene
small brown girl gets asked will she perform a play for them
so she writes angry, clever, funny
draws them in then spits them out
but afterwards
she thanks them for the opportunity
a justification for being here
a receipt to prove she's not lost

small brown girl thinks it's funny to say *thank you*
when she still performs to a red jaw full of white teeth
she asks her friend to come watch her
friend says *I don't really care about theatre*

small brown girl wonders if that's the same as
how her friend works full-time
how her other friend has a two-year old child and cleans part-time
how her other friend lives too far out of town
how her grandma has bad knees
how her sister hates feeling like she's under a microscope
and doesn't feel comfortable in spaces bigger than the living room

small brown girl doesn't really care about theatre either
people tell small brown girl
you must write stories for the stage
but small brown girl wants to ask, for who?
her friends are all at home.

small brown girl stands in a red jaw full of white teeth
dressed her best but not good enough
pretends she is not affronted by the price of ice cream
pretends this is not a birthday gift
pretends those are not border-guards
pretends
pretends
plays pretend
pretending
      this
         could ever be for her

This poem was a commission for the International Theatre
Engineering and Architecture Conference – one of the more obscure
conferences I have been commissioned for. The prompt was around
the accessibility of theatres and my own experience with theatre. To
write the poem I reflected on my (at the time) recent experience of
being asked to write a play for Theatre Uncut despite having little to no
experience in theatre and therefore the imposter syndrome that came
with this. But I also asked friends and peers for their experiences and
feelings on the question and thus the anecdotes and experiences in the
poem are an amalgamation of different people of colours' experiences
in total.

DECENTERING DIVERSITY

Equal access to unjust systems is not liberation
More people of colour on pedagogically unchanged reading lists
is not salvation, and no number of black and brown faces in
universities can fundamentally undo the racism

Just because they give you a seat at the table
doesn't mean they want you to speak at the table

It's a virtuous invitation that reflects well on the host
and the only thing that's better than a generous institution
is a grateful beneficiary who'll follow the key rule:
that people of colour should be seen and not heard
(fit for open-day handbooks but not safety in academia)

Equal access to unjust systems is not liberation
More people of colour on pedagogically unchanged reading lists
is not salvation, and no number of black and brown faces in
universities can fundamentally undo the racism

Just because they give you a seat at the table
doesn't mean they want you to eat at the table

They make out that the racism is the number of students of colour
but not that it's the underestimation of their knowledge
the exclusion of their histories and distortion of their names
the policing of their speech and a culture of surveillance

They make out that the racism is the content of core modules
but not that it's that whiteness is the mark of valued knowledge
the processes that underlie the racist drop-out rate
or the lack of mental health services that can understand race

Just because they give you a seat at the table
doesn't mean that they'll take their feet off the table

They make out that the racism is the number of academics of colour
but not that it's the treatment of the other black and brown staff
the cleaners and the caterers, the security on the door
not that it's the fees or the opaque decision-making

Equal access to unjust systems is not liberation
More people of colour on pedagogically unchanged reading lists
is not salvation, and no number of black and brown faces in
universities can fundamentally undo the racism

Just because they give you a seat at the table
doesn't mean they're prepared to change the room

I wrote this poem as a commission for the 'Decentring Diversity Symposium'
held at Brunel University on 25 March 2019, organised by Broderick Chow,
Sarita Malik, Royona Mitra and Serene Natile. The symposium aimed to
interrogate the way that whilst Universities have made vocal efforts towards
"diversity", the structural inequalities which prompted calls for "diversity" in
the first place remain largely unaddressed. My poem for the symposium tried
to explore that irony using the 'seat at the table' metaphor that is often used
to discuss the needs of excluded and marginalised people. Is a 'seat at the
table' (e.g. diversity) actually what we want? Is representation the
antithesis of oppression? I don't think so, transforming the conditions of
structural violence, exclusion and inequality that exist within institutions has
to be done actively and holistically with a focus to changing not only who sits
at the table but the table, chairs and very notion of the room.

5

Q: "WHAT DOES IT MEAN TO BE A MUSLIM WOMAN?"

To be a Muslim woman is to never speak for oneself
to never exist for oneself, but for everyone else
to know that even when you speak you are not heard unless it fits
the narrative
to exist only to justify your existence.

To be a Muslim woman is to be asked but already decided
a political pawn
a justification for invasion
a weapon to strike against Islam.

It is to be always an object
object of fascination: veiled body
object of desire: mystery body
object of ridicule: letterbox body [*]
always an object.

To be a Muslim woman is to be represented or representative
but never real
even to 'correct' 'misrepresentation' you are reduced to other
representations.

To be a Muslim woman is to be picture but never painter
to be surreal, uncanny, not-quite
to be an outsider to yourself: a conversation, a joke, a jibe.

---

[*] In the summer of 2018, Boris Johnson, former Conservative Party Foreign Secretary and always racist, made the dehumanising, objectifying, misogynistic, Islamophobic and criminalising comments that women who wore burkas looked like "letterboxes" and "bank robbers".

It is to be always already framed
to be made excruciatingly small and impossibly big at once
to be swallowed and vomited out at the same time.

To be a Muslim woman is to be always fought over
but never fought for.

'SCHOOL INSPECTORS IN ENGLAND HAVE BEEN TOLD TO START ASKING YOUNG GIRLS IN PRIMARY SCHOOL WHY THEY ARE WEARING A HIJAB IN ORDER TO ASCERTAIN IF THEY ARE BEING SEXUALISED.'

for Ofsted

you say you care about Muslim girls as if you care about the
Muslim women they are standing in the pasts of

you say you care about the sexualisation of Muslim girls as if you do
not turn a blind eye to the rise of Islamophobic misogyny which sees
cries like "give us a flash" levelled at women in hijab and niqab

you say you care about the sexualisation of Muslim girls as if you care
about the sexualisation of girls
as if you do not facilitate the categorisation of the sexual future of
babies lives when you reduce them to *girl*

you say you care about the sexualisation of Muslim girls as if we are
victims of parents who are simultaneously sexually repressed and
hypersexual
not so different from your colonial fantasies of us as sensual
eastern mysteries as well as suicide bomber threats

you say you care about Muslim girls
but you place our victimhood in our selves
so keen to save us from our Muslimness that you distract from your
own investment in our patriarchal domination

you pretend little girls are safe when their heads are uncovered
as if paedophilia is not endemic in this society
as if human trafficking is as underground as it is made out to be
as if billboard ads and television shows don't insist on the
sexualisation of girls from birth
as if you don't envision the sexual and marital futures of your
babies from the moment go

you say you care about Muslim girls
because you care about how we dress

but you do not care about Muslim girls when we are burning
you do not care about Muslim girls when we are screaming
you do not care about Muslim girls when we are drowning
when we are neglected
when we are at your borders
when we are starving
when we are in detention centres waiting for deportation
when we are in the bodies of mothers in detention centres waiting
for deportation
when we are outspoken
asking for accountability for your war crimes
for recognition of our humanity
you do not care about Muslim girls when you bomb them into
drone-democracy, rape, and death

you do not care about Muslim girls when we are asking

we are symbolic signifiers for you
a way to talk about something else
and your concern for our sexualisation
is a way to stop talking about everything else

our bodies are monuments to be covered or uncovered
depending what the exhibition is called this time
will it be: *Feminist reasons to extend the surveillance state?*
or: *Reasons white supremacy must not be addressed as patriarchy?*

do not say you care about Muslim girls when you care only to
make out we are Other
pretending our lives are completely incomprehensible
that our shadowy household activities can only be relayed
through the mouths of babes

you do not care about Muslim girls
because you do not care about girls or Muslims

so do not tell me you care about the sexualisation of Muslim girls
until you care about your investment in it

In November 2017, the chief of Ofsted, the school inspectorate service in
the UK, announced that school inspectors should 'start asking young girls
in primary school why they are wearing a hijab in order to ascertain if they
are being sexualised'. The news was absurd and undeniably
discriminatory, based in a clear assumption of a specific and exceptional
levels of misogyny inherent to Muslims – symbolised by the motif of the
hijab. Many pointed out that Muslim school children are already
targeted and Othered and this policy would further this, questions were
raised around free will, religious freedoms, the policing of girl's dress
choices and the way children at primary school age often wear a range
of clothes based on imitation – where the imitation may be of someone
wearing a headscarf this was now being deemed automatically
problematic; where schools demand girls wear skirts/skirts of a certain
length should this not also be deemed sexualisation? Where is the line and
why the double standard? And how did this fall under Ofsted's remit?

This poem was my take on the issue which looks less at countering the
claim itself but trying to reveal the function that the claim in question has.
What is made possible by asserting that young girls should be asked why

they are wearing hijab? Well, in this case since the government clearly doesn't care about Muslim women's wellbeing in any other regard (what about poverty? what about the fact almost 50% of Muslims in the UK live in the top 10% most deprived council areas? employment discrimination? disproportionate levels of imprisonment? the impact of austerity? Islamophobic policing enabled by government policy like Prevent and gendered islamophobia garnered by media rhetoric?) I argue that this pretend concern over us being sexualised from a young age is bound up with the historical focus on Muslim women as a way to Other and regulate Muslim populations.

If you can co-opt Muslim women, conceptually you are co-opting/ controlling Muslim families and children – e.g. the next generation of Muslims. Since the visibility of Muslim women was historically so bound up with colonisation and conquest – e.g. unveiling ceremonies held by the French in Algeria, or even more contemporarily the 'unveiling' of an Afghan woman by Oprah Winfrey after the invasion of Afghanistan – Muslim women covering their bodies has always been deemed problematic and an indicator of an inability to properly control or assimilate Muslim populations. Concern with Muslim women's dress is therefore never benign or sincerely about relieving us from patriarchal domination – if it was then there would need to be a shift to focus on the latent white supremacist patriarchy that harms all women of colour and Muslim women. Faux concern over how girls dress is a way to displace and obscure the problems Muslim women and girls face that are caused by anyone other than Muslim men – the government, state and institutions do not have to be held to account for being so deeply invested in our oppression, and in patriarchy.

For more watch my TEDx talk on this topic – 'I'm bored of talking about Muslim women'.

PICK ONE

for the woman who asked

Muslim, Feminist, or Human?
pick One
she drawls
says One like it's a knife
says One like I might fall
One with a loose O
a noose big enough for a small neck

Muslim, Feminist, or Human?
I sterile laugh at the boxes
watch her eyes watch me
know this
is a trick
a question especially selected
which mask will I choose?
no matter so long as it's not niqab

I sterile laugh at the boxes
say *that's absurd - a false distinction!*
she catches that with two hands
kind eye clinically informs me
that word - absurd - is very patronising

I wonder if she has ever been patronised
wonder if she has ever been asked to split herself
to reverse algebra
make her body a sum of parts
make herself less

Muslim, Feminist, or Human?
the wrong answer would be Muslim
I know this.
to see myself foremostly as a soul in submission
to see myself foremostly as beyond this life
to see myself foremostly in reference to Allah
to see myself foremostly as unable to see

the right answer would be Human
I know this.
to see myself foremostly as Just like Her
to see myself foremostly as Citizen
to see myself foremostly as Nation-State
to see myself foremostly as she does not see me

I wonder how that word tastes on her tongue
whatever lies taste like I'm sure
how can I give an answer that denies me?
how can I accept a label that doesn't stick?

Human until you're not
Universal Rights until they're not
conditional clauses for skins a shade less than worthy

her eyes search my face
I search for a way out
to say Feminist is to reduce myself to her whims
she will read it as *save me*
she will read it as *guilty*
she will read it as *afraid*

all the while I know her feminism is not for me
she wants to uncover me without seeing me
unwrap me only for the glimpse

pick One she drawls
says One like it's a knife

pick One she drawls
says One like I might fall

pick One she drawls
One with a loose O
a noose big enough for a small neck

but won't you try it on with me, sister?
cut your human wrists with mine?
bathe in this colourless blood we share

after all
we are not at war, are we?

we are not at war, are we?

you are not holding a noose between your teeth
you are not making an offering of me

are you, sister?

sorry – I don't mean to patronise!

IF A GIRL CRIES IN A CORRIDOR AND NO-ONE IS THERE TO SEE IT WAS SHE EVEN IN PAIN?

[a commission for Maslaha]

They are all skinny ankles
baggy sweatshirts
and trousers too short
close birth dates shoved in the same washing machine
and come out in jumbled sizes

But despite these differences
all carry the expectations
of the women they're meant to grow into
like the hyperbole bags on their backs:
ill-fitting and not made for children

Politicians say letterbox
news says hate crime statistic or danger level increase
internet says ripped off hijab
independent report says underachieving
policy reviews say aspiration-needing
stranger says housewife
man on the street says object of his pleasure
society says problem person needing to be policed

Under that mocking weight you'd think they'd never laugh
but they are all smiles
hands holding back chortles on baby faces
and big eyes offering grins
grins that stay two sizes bigger than
the expectant jaws of a world wanting to eat them up in its definitions

They know the rules already
have been listening since the moment they were birthed
already know the playground is tilted
that the classrooms are minefields
and the walk home just gets longer every day

Which is to say
they already know their world is unsafe
they already know that if they don't have their own backs no one will
cos they know their bodies are coded betrayal
know they'll be burnt at the stake whether they cover or uncover

know 'girls don't play sport' means white girls don't play sport
other girls don't really count as girls at all
girls of colour barely exist
Muslim girls are so visible they're invisible

'cos the line between blinding and being overlooked is thin

If a girl cries in a corridor and no one is there to see it
was she really in pain?

If a girl drowns in society's assumptions and we don't notice
did she even deserve to thrive?

What is the myth of pulling yourself up by your bootstraps in such a
perilous playground?
What becomes of education when you can learn the most important
lessons out of school?
What does it mean when no one will protect you?

These girl's names slip off registers easily
get murmured into obscurity

but they will not

They are metaphors that refuse to be someone else's poem
in a world where everyone wants to define them
but never give them the pen
their words are revolutions
their speech is protest
and their laughter
is a relentless refusal to be confined
to other people's mouths

FUNERAL OF THE AUTHENTIC MUSLIM WOMAN

Dearly beloved
we are gathered here today to bury the memory of the one
who never was

who was written by others
made for others
and imposed on us

Today
let us stamp on her grave and the world she was made to hold us in

This is for the girls who cover their hair in the mornings and hang it
loose by night
for the girls who keep it covered and those who never do
for the girls who were forced to, those forced not to
and those whose parents made no comment
the ones who wear it loose, wear it barely, wear it groovy
the ones who don't know why they wear it
the ones who only sometimes do
the anti-capitalist male-gaze resisters
the sisters who remind us hijab does not mean cloth
the taking-it-off-on-days-after-attack
the wearing-it-in-bolder-colours
the more-than-their-wearing-it
the consumed-by-their-wearing-it
the worn by it
weary with it
worn and war-torn with it

Dearly beloved
this is for the women who've been spat at for their faith
who've had people cross the road over their faith
who've had buses filled with hate over their faith
and the ones not noted as connected on the bus
the overlooked as ones
the asked-if-they're-drinkers
and the drinkers

those who do what the boys do and better
who denounce the boys
who are the boys
are better than the boys
who love the boys
are loved by the boys
wish they had the freedom of the boys
steal the freedom of *their* boys
stand for the freedom of the boys
don't vilify the boys
are vilified by the boys and still stand for their rights

Dearly beloved
this is for the girls who learnt their bodies meant shame before they
learnt anything else
for the girls who shave off the shame and the girls who own it
for the secret relationships, the secret bodies, the embodied secrets
the silent babies, the never born, the accidentally had
the quickly covered up, the unjustly touched, the unafraid
the naked skin, the hypocritical kiss, the closed legs
the afraid to touch and the never touched

Dearly beloved
this is for the married and the unmarried
the never-married and the soon-to-be-married
the unmarriageable, the second-marriage, the anti-marriage
the marriage conversation, the wedding day dream
the one for-our-parents, the runaway bride
the marriage mistake and the happy divorce

Dearly beloved
this is for the sisters who wake consistently at dawn and those who
never can
for the prayer-sharing and the sleep-defying
the sometimes-waking and the sleepy
the ones who stumble over the words
the ones who know the entire book and the ones who struggle with it

for the ones who get five times a day
the ones who get five minutes a night
the ones whose five-year-old brings them back to the book
the five-pound translation, the translator, the educator
the student, and the mum

Dearly beloved
this is for the quiet girls and the ones who speak too much
the spoken for and the spoken over
the girls who speak for the girls
who speak wrongly for the girls
who think they can speak for the girls
and the girls who don't speak
are sick of speaking, already spoke, spent too long woke
whose words are lost
whose voice is hoarse
and those still shouting

We were always here and *she* never was

So when two hands offer us either: victimhood, or the total refusal of it
may we find comfort in our own hands
may we find comfort in the space between our hands
where cameras never flash and stories do not weave themselves

for we were always here and she never was

So today
let us stamp on her grave and the world she was made to hold us in

---

I wrote this poem as a commission for TEDxYouth@Brum held in Birmingham, 2017. The theme of the conference was 'Courage'. This poem felt courageous because it was a refusal and denunciation of the idea that there is an 'authentic' Muslim Woman. It rejects others' attempts to define who the "real" Muslim woman is: against media representations of 'real' Muslim women as oppressed, against politicians expressing that 'real' Muslim women deserve policing, against other Muslims' expectations of Muslim women having to embody piety in certain ways to count as 'genuinely' Muslim, it goes against expectations and frames made by anyone about what a Muslim woman is or should be and about who gets to be one or counted as one.

However, in rejecting those definition this poem also refuses to simply say "we are not oppressed", or "we are not what you think we are" and fall into the simple binary of liberated vs oppressed. The truth is much more nuanced, and we deserve to be allowed to exist in our multifacetedness. To focus always on "breaking stereotypes" is to rely on them just as much as perpetuating them. This poem is a rejection of the idea that Muslim women should have to define ourselves in reference to any external standard or that anyone but a Muslim woman herself can decide what her authenticity looks like.

I believe Muslim women are Muslim women if they say they are and that no one has any right to question that or tell them what that looks like or tell them they aren't good enough or can't count as one. This poem stands in the face of the way Muslim women are most often just a bartering tool that different groups use to symbolise and claim their own goals – e.g. to say Muslims are sexist, to say childcare should be solely women's labour, to displace problems of misogyny, vulnerable youth, social issues and male egos. It unapologetically embraces the multiplicity and contradictory ways there are of being a Muslim woman. We will not be boxed or split or spoken for.

RECLAIM THE NIGHT

[written for Reclaim the Night march, Cambridge, 2015]

Tonight
we will reclaim it all

reclaim the silver starlight from the skies
weave it into ropes
which we will use to take back the silence of 2am
seize the darkness of cobbled streets

Tonight
we will reclaim it all

we will pluck the pavements back from the arms of entitled
looming shadows
we will snatch back the feeling of solitude in open fields
we will recover the art of confidence even where the street lights flicker

we will become the flickers

we will create every shadow
we will be the night
and the night will be us

Tonight
we will reclaim every gust that blows
let our voices carry
un-hushed
un-hurried

we will unfurl our fear
trace it out on maps
we will lose the maps
and walk

Tonight we will walk
but we will reclaim the art of walking
we will stride
march
stamp
heads high
rescue our eyes from the ground
and our ears
from the footsteps
always the footsteps

we will be visible
heard

but we will also reclaim our right not to be

Tonight
we will salvage hesitance
and empower purposelessness
Tonight
we will reclaim it all

not just the night
not just the space
Tonight we will reclaim it all

each of us
she will grasp back the trees
claim the darkened parks
embrace every bit of shade
swallow it whole
feel the moonlight kiss our skins
devour the stars
consume the skies
exhaust the road beneath our feet

Tonight
we will reclaim the night
and she
she will be free

DIDN'T YOU KNOW?

Didn't you know white men invented everything?
his rotting breath
spills into my side of the room
as he explains to me
my humanity

He extracts my limbs
from his teeth
and deconstructs me on the table
amidst cheeses I can't pronounce
as if I too
can be consumed
and finished off
in the next round

He deconstructs and dissects
in the same way they did so many continents
probably on tables just like this

But didn't I know white men invented everything?
they didn't deconstruct
they constructed
continents didn't exist
without their toilet paper touch

I am not there
I am never there
I am not real outside of his gorged and purpling lips

Should I thank him then
for mentioning me?
for legitimising my existence?

He leans forward
as he does another white man comes into view
a portrait just above his head
a mirror image minus several hundred years

'You shouldn't talk only about race' he tells me
'you have to consider gender too'
I don't know what to say in response
he wants a back pat
for having just invented me
for having just created categories to fit my existence into

but his invention of me is my undoing

I cannot now exist outside his mind
I am boxed
I am trapped
I am being contained

contained in the same way that borders
are just pen marks on paper
but also they are pain

and in boxing me
he splits me
segments me
and takes my voice

It used to be a joke that I couldn't finish my sentences
that I was always ready to be cut off
ready to be talked over
ready to be ignored

It used to be a joke that there was silence
because nobody listens to silence

He tells me I am abstract
not one thing
but a series of disjointed reports
not real
just skin

Didn't you know white men invented everything?
the boxes I am in
are not my own
and the words of this poem
are the only ones I know
but not the ones I chose to learn

Didn't you know white men invented everything?
I look in the mirror
and ask if I really know me
if anyone does
because whose performance am I?
and in what cage do I belong?

I cannot talk only about race
but I cannot talk of gender too
for I am not two things
I am one

but didn't I know white men invented everything?
the art of talking
the art of being one
they will lie to you that you cannot exist outside their mouths
and thus you must come in bitesize chunks
palatable

But he doesn't know
that I have invented him
he is only white because I am not
and he is man because he calls me woman

I have invented him
not because I need him, only to make a point
but he
he cannot forsake me
for to forsake me is to forsake part of his white self
that is so visible he thinks it is invisible
that he thinks race and gender apply only to me

weapons in his hands
they dissolve in mine

I am not there
it is he who is
he imagines me so he can breathe
he invents me so I cannot

Sometimes a poem is not enough because it is only words
and sometimes a poem is too much because it is words
but it is somewhere to exist, outside their mouths

I wrote 'Didn't You Know' during my time studying History at the University of Cambridge. It is also published in the book I co-wrote, *A FLY GIRL'S GUIDE TO UNIVERSITY: Being a woman of colour at Cambridge and other institutions of power and elitism*, 2019.

20 POINT MANIFESTO FOR WOMEN LIVING IN GENOCIDAL TIMES

1. Ask which women just came to your mind.

2. Ask which women did not just come to your mind.

3. Look in the mirror
   know you are not all of us
   know you are one of us
   know the genocidal times began long before you
   though.

4. Know you are not your body but your body is yours
   so kiss the mirror sometimes
   even if it is cracked - especially if it is cracked.

   Do not wait to become a fashionable trend
   it is faster just to love yourself.

5. Do not believe the exhibitions.
   100 years for who?
   Some women stood on the round darker bellies of others
   just to get a taste of the pie.

   Know there were feminists before their feminism
   there was history before Europe
   "progress" before
   "progressive values" were coerced onto the world
   there were working mothers before there was applause
   there were fields and bending knees and factory night-
   shifts and silence

for the history of the world is not a history of Great Men
or Nation-States
or Civilisations
or Wars
it is a history of women.

6. Do not want equality with men whose power comes from
   their subjugation of others
   wish for more than being the other side of the joke
   wish for more than putting someone else into the
   capitalist punchline
   for more than making cracks about small hands and
   orange skin.

   If it takes emasculation to bring down the ones in power
   then we concede that being less 'man'
   is being humiliated
   and being more 'woman' is being a joke.

7. The master's tools will never destroy the master's house
   after all
   women CEOs don't mean much for the women working
   for them in low-wage, precarious, life-threatening
   conditions.

8. Do not go alone.

9. Do not go alone.

10. There is always space for everyone.
    There is no reason we must queue for freedom
    some women perpetually at the back
    it is all or nothing
    so stand in a row instead.

11. You do not have to climb over me to climb upwards.
    Hold hands with the women you don't know
    not just the ones you respect
    not just the ones you don't avert your eyes from
    not just the ones you get.
    You do not have to climb over me to climb upwards.

12. Do not let yourself be reduced
    they will try to split you
    look for more than representation
    call for reparation.

13. Ask the questions that scare you
    ask if the liberals are really so different from the fascists?

    The liberals will say they stand for freedom of speech
    whilst restricting what Muslims can talk about
    the fascists will cut our tongues out instead.

    But what's the difference when we're silenced?

    What's the difference when it still means a drone
    dropped on your home?
    What's the difference when you're still in Guantanamo
    Bay?
    What's the difference when you're tortured?
    What's the difference when your body is still suspect?
    What's the difference when we're dead?

14. Liberation is not a door that opens from the inside
    do not wait
    do not ask permission dress up pretty blink your eyes
    and ask to be let in,
    kick it down.

15. Realise liberation is not a door at all,
    not something you walk through and enter
    but something that's in you
    your sharp tongue, big heart and weeping eyes.

16. Liberation did not come from the ballot box.
    Liberation will not come from the government.
    Know the state will placate you as it dehumanises you.
    Know "women's rights" only count if they see you first as
    "woman".

    There are women who will never be "woman".
    They are sitting in refugee camps
    in detention centres and under rubble.

    They will tell you these women were victims to their own
    societies
    had they only made it to the West they would have been
    free
    like you,
    had you only invaded their countries to save them they
    would have been free
    like you,

    know you are not free.

    Know this is only progress the way wrapping a rope
    around your own neck gets you closer to death.

17. Know that genitals aren't necessary to bring us together.
    The revolution doesn't need to be pink.
    The reclamation doesn't need to be naked.
    What makes us oppressed is not that we are the same
    but that we are in pain.

18. Do not be afraid of the questioning,
    just because it feels bad doesn't mean it is
    wonder if your comfort is more important than her
    freedom.

19. Do not point over the ocean to say it is worse in America.
    We are killing the darker ones here too
    we just let them die under suspicious circumstances in
    custody rather than outright assassinate them on the
    street.

    We are separating the babies from their families here, too
    we just hide it better and point the camera elsewhere.

    We are killing civilians overseas here, too
    we just sell the bombs for others to do the dropping.

    We are barricading the border here, too.
    We are surveiling the Muslims here, too.
    We are murdering the marginalised here, too.
    We are groping the women here, too.
    We are excluding, dehumanising and destroying.

20. Fight.
    Love uncompromisingly.
    Hone your weapon - your voice, your hands.
    Go forward and grasp,
    but do not go alone,
    you won't make it alone,
    we won't make it.

    Come together - you too
    it won't be easy,
    but we were trained for that,

    we are women, after all.

I performed this poem for the first time at the Anti-Trump Women's March in 2018. It came out of my outrage at both the violent racist misogyny myself and those I love face, as well as my outrage at the violent racism, exclusiveness and hypocrisy of the women's movement in Britain in its response to Trump. All violence and injustice has to be eradicated for women to be free – this isn't about a single-issue struggle or a simplistic notion of 'equality', or even about displacing all problems onto Trump and the USA, this is about facing up to the pervasiveness of structural oppression, historic injustice and the inherent violence of nation-states. I therefore wrote this manifesto as both a rallying call and a caution to the audience I anticipated would hear it at the march.

MAYBE I DON'T

I want men who cry like thunder
who step out of their glass forms
and burn
phoenix into blossom
like roses in their own cheeks
and who smile like the sun leaking in your window

men who have no eyes
and tongues made fearless
say 'beautiful' of other men
and cannot form fists with hands at all

I want men who condemn
not shameful eyes on floor
awkward grin elbow to rib
men who know no maps
and leave like sunsets

I want men who love like spilling coffee on their shirts
who laugh like wisdom
and shatter again and again

I want men who aren't
who hatch full adult into static white noise
who can't tell hand from shoulder

men before man is moulded
men more like women
women more like men
mothering men
sisterly men
beards like pearly necklaces

big as the sun
and just as brightly burn

I want sincerity
men unmasked
unafraid of the warmth of sand beneath their feet
dragged out of the soil
gnarled like ancient trees
born before the ocean
consumed by time

so maybe I don't

6

STRADDLING THE / LINE
you'll know if it's for you

they want to know me to pigeon hole me
but I am a key with too many nooks
I make slippery surfaces of stop signs

lay your traps out like dichotomies and I will overturn the table
ask if I'm moderate or radical
I'll ask what made you think your dictionary was universal
what made you think you were the only author?
what made you think I'd shake either of those hands?

and if I don't shake hands

you ask
am I more liberal or traditional?
I'll ask what made you think my submission was time bound?
what made you think you could string the nights and days
with modern on one end and me on the other?
what made you think I'd want your past or present?

I am my own temporality
I am heartbeats flamencoing to southern jazz
to the cheers of the revolters
to the sound of the revolver

they want me small enough to fit a word but
I am manuscripts
I am archives
I am the libraries they tried to burn down

if all the oceans were ink
they would run dry before the words of my Creator did

and I am of those

mightier than all the measures they construct
for hands on clocks have nothing on death

which is to say
bricks, mortar, steel and iron
cannot stop the ocean

for you cannot control what was never yours

which is to say

I will never be yours

A VIRTUE OF DISOBEDIENCE

[commissioned & inspired by Asim Qureshi's book by the same name]

We are the disobedient
look upon us and despair
for we outlast history, time, and memory
we are always there

We are the unquenchable thirst for justice
the bodies that do not bend
tongues you cannot straightjacket
and eyes that will not be turned blind

We are the step you trip on in the night
the nightmare you wake from but cannot recall
the lump under the rolling hill that reminds you what is buried there

We are the disobedient
We bear witness and we testify
We love despite the lie that we are not worthy
We hold despite being told we should hide

Yes - we are the disobedient
who refuse to die
for bodies without eulogies will never remain in their graves
we are the ghosts of the unmourned
and the spirits of the never-grieved

We are the original traitors to the tireless tyrant

We are Mohammed
We are Malcolm
We are Moses and Assata
We are Toussaint and Bhashani
We are Rosa and Rabbani
We are the disobedient

Truth-speakers with tongues of fire
knowledge seekers who provoke your ire
mouths always moist from sincere prayer

We are hearts beating for the truth
not like fluttering birds in cages
but like the earth in her final convulsions
like mountains when they scatter to dust
we dismantle, uproot, expose

We are the disobedient
and we have come not to claim what is yours
but what is and always was ours:
our humanity

But no – not claim
for it was always with us
and our announcement of that
is the blasphemy you burn us for

But there's a reason you mustn't play with fire
'cos the flames are not bound by only your aims
if you burn our bodies in the morning
the fire will be licking your heels that night

Do you feel secure then?
When we are bound not by law, but justice?
Loyal not to pen mark on paper, but truth?

We are unconquerable and unmanageable
because you can take what you want
if all you want is to take

We are your greatest fear: fearless
loyal not even to life
There is no bargain to be made then
for disruption is our only security
in a world which says security is ensured only through our
repression - what basis has such authority to be obeyed?

No - we are the disobedient
who refuse to know our place
undivided, low, and mighty

we are a We
a unity, a community
a principle above place

We are the disobedient
we declare the emperor naked
and don't kneel before the queen
we smash the idols
confront the Pharaoh
upend the fabric of the world
we will not sell our souls for hallowed halls
we cannot be unmoved

We are the disobedient
we overspill and overspeak
we are unboxed, unharnessed, unfathomable
unpalatable
uncompromising

Oh Ozymandiases of the world
do you really think yourselves kings of kings?
how quickly you forget
nothing outlasts the fading of the day
but the light of truth itself

This poem was written as a commission for Asim Qureshi's
incredible book, *A Virtue of Disobedience*, which makes the case
that standing for justice and truth even when and where it means
you're 'disobeying' or 'disrupting' is an Islamic duty. The
references to names are the following: the Prophet Muhammad
(SAW), Malcolm X, Prophet Moses (AS), Assata Shakur (black
revolutionary), Toussaint Louverture (leader of the Haitian
revolution), Maulana Bhashani (anti-colonial resistance leader
in what is now Bangladesh), Rosa Parks (black revolutionary and
activist), Mohammed Rabbani (activist and leader).

BACON, BANKNOTES, BENJAMINS

[a commission for R.A.P Party]

Bacon, Banknotes, Benjamins,
Cheddar, Cheese, Dead Presidents,
Fetti, Franklins, Gs and Greens,
Lincolns, Moola, Pesos, Ps

It's all about the m-m-m-m-m
less about the shimmy shimmy ya shimmy yay

like, Jay-Z says he's not a businessman
he's a business, man
and to let him handle his business, damn

but isn't being a 'business, man'
not too far from being a product?
and isn't being a product on the road to being sold?
and isn't that exactly what was rapped about
before aiming for platinum and gold?

'cos it seems to me that from fighting the power
we've gone to *climbing* that tower
and freedom's been appropriated as buying brand attire
freedom of the people, rebranded as a market
its Pinochet again, but in lyrical format [5]

---

[5] Pinochet was the dictator of Chile between 1973-90 after a US-backed
military coup overthrowing the democratically elected government. The
military dictatorship implemented economic liberalisation including
privatisation and banning trade unions, rounding up socialists and leftists.

'cos the corporate capturing of a critical sub-culture
then selling it back to people of colour
as Apple, Samsung, Nike and Chrysler
is not so different from the conquest of our lands
private exploitation of resources from our hands
raw materials taken then sold back to us for profit
just as messages of subversion have been rebranded for the market

but I guess it's easier to celebrate the mass consumption of hip-hop
than to ask who's generating the wealth and is actually on top
and making the

Bacon, Banknotes, Benjamins,
Cheddar, Cheese, Dead Presidents,
Fetti, Franklins, Gs and Greens,
Lincolns, Moola, Pesos, Ps

Formerly freedom fermented in street parties
a way to gain power as a disenfranchised culture
but now it seems power-gaining is the culture
no more emphasis on free-thinking for liberation
the critiques are only woke enough to pass for entertainment

not woke enough that they're consequential
not like Zulu Nation's revolutionary potential
now freedom is framed firstly as financial fixation
the freedom to consume not socio-political emancipation

So the outcome is still the same for the majority
most racialised people still face intergenerational poverty
to avert the problem we're told
keep up the grind so you can wine and dine
- capitalism's apparent silver-lining

but grinding is rap language for
"pull yourselves up by your bootstraps"
ignoring that our boots are being worn on others' feet
and very few people are still rapping about that feat
and that cheat that means

the same people are incarcerated
there's a social housing crisis and surveillance state
the ghettos are still ghettos
the consumers are still marginalised
the only thing that's changed is that the genre has been gentrified
for the sake of the

Bacon, Banknotes, Benjamins,
Cheddar, Cheese, Dead Presidents,
Fetti, Franklins, Gs and Greens,
Lincolns, Moola, Pesos, Ps

My outlining the co-option of hip-hop by capitalism
is not just condemnation, but a speculation
about whether hip-hop is not just a metaphor
for the marketization of all resistance

the consumption of our other messages:
t-shirts about being feminist, made by women in sweat-shop
factories,
anti-capitalist as an aesthetic vibe, liberals buying clothes for double
their price,
ally as a hashtag used by allies who moved out of our neighbourhoods,
and Californian-avocado-eating-vegans wasting water on avocado
growth

The techniques of resistance have never been so mortal
from the decentralised screams of the dispossessed
to modern day accumulation by dispossession

soon enough Kanye will rap about Decolonising the University
Snoop will ask you to "queer" your cookbook
Jay-Z subvert your wardrobe
and Drake your bed

cos there's nothing more alarming
than poor people of colour claiming power
but nothing so easily disarming
as misdirecting us towards only the

Bacon, Banknotes, Benjamins,
Cheddar, Cheese, Dead Presidents,
Fetti, Franklins, Gs and Greens,
Lincolns, Moola, Pesos, Ps

P P P PREVENT

you cannot say that you're Preventing terrorists
if all that you're doing is pre-empting terrorists

'cos in a political climate where terror is presupposed in Muslim
people
your predictions are predicated purely on profiling
and this premise of profiling lacks scientific precision
it just takes perceived Muslimness as the prerequisite for violent
decisions

so whilst pre-emption might sound like it makes political sense
in a legal system that purports to presume innocence
Prevent is nothing more than prejudice

'cos now a beard, or a penchant for the wrong Prophet, or praying
become proof of a predisposition to political violence you're
displaying
yet the polemics of politicians who protest Muslim presence
don't qualify as Prevent-worthy practices requiring repentance

so what we're looking at is public policy prepared prior to evidence
that even the psychologists have said is pseudoscience
a project that promotes the policing of Muslim people
placing pressure on the public sector to presume Muslim pupils and
patients are prone to evil

you cannot say that you're Preventing terrorists
if all that you're doing is pre-empting terrorists

and to argue it's okay cos Prevent also prevents far-right extremists
is to lie that a system predicated on Islamophobic prejudice
could possibly protect Muslims from a persecuting legislative

it is to lie that policy based in predictive policing could possibly
be used to Prevent itself

that providing further profit to an Islamophobic project
is not just the most palpable manifestation
of state persecution made publicly palatable through
institutionalisation

and let's not pretend Prevent has no purpose either
cos promoting the presumption that Muslims are prone to violence
conveniently pretends that the state cannot be violent
no need to ponder the parameters that shape Muslim lives
no puzzling over foreign or domestic policy, arms trades, or racial
profiling

see, Prevent perpetuates public policy participating in displacement
protecting the state and government from any pertinent debasement
no need to hold the political infrastructures accountable
instead the problem is Muslims and the Muslim problem is
insurmountable

Pretty convenient no?

you cannot say that you're Preventing terrorists
if all that you're doing is pre-empting terrorists

perhaps if instead of Prevent we could ponder the past that made
political violence probable
but imperialism loves to pretend itself away
so police are given more powers as if policing protects the nation
and prisons and deportation planes are methods of purgation

in the end Prevent is nothing but political deflection
proof that the state is headed in the most authoritarian direction

so prepare for permanent conditions of political persecution
'cos even if it's not yet palpable to you
the project of resistance is your obligation, too
the project of resistance is your obligation, too

'Prevent' refers to the Prevent Duty which is a part of CONTEST, the UK government's 'strategy for countering terrorism'. CONTEST includes four 'P' strands – Prevent, Protect, Pursue and Prepare (that inspired the poem's focus on P-words). The Prevent strand of CONTEST is the one that this poem focuses on. In the government's point of view, Prevent is focused on 'stopping people from becoming terrorists or supporting terrorism'. It was initially introduced in 2003 but the policy became a legal duty for all public sector institutions in 2015. This has meant that since 2015, anybody who works in schools, Universities, councils, hospitals and other public service institutions (more than 50,000 public servants) is legally bound to 'look out for signs of radicalisation' amongst people they interact with from students to patients.

As a policy, Prevent has been widely condemned for stigmatising Muslims and creating a mass surveillance system by requiring every public servant to treat Muslims with the suspicion that they may "become terrorists" and need to be watched for "signs" of this. Over 150 academics and psychologists have critiqued Prevent for these reasons and for the fact that the evidence that underpins the policy has never been subject to proper scientific scrutiny or public critique. The scientific study that Prevent is supposedly based on (the 'Extreme Risk Guidance 22+ framework') is classified, that means it cannot be accessed by the public and researchers at CAGE found that 'the authors of the study recognise [it] cannot be used as a predictive tool' – however, it has been used as such in the underpinning of Prevent.

My poem sums up this and many other problems with Prevent and why it must ultimately be resisted and abolished. For me, the most harmful element is the way it works to make anybody assumed to be Muslim into a suspect. The radicalisation thesis assumes that any Muslim could become 'radical' and therefore all Muslims require treating with suspicion. This theory is completely flawed because it assumes that the cause of violence is something lying dormant in Muslims that could be triggered at any moment, or a specific 'Muslim ideology' (e.g. Islam). Such an understanding of ideological or innate propensity to violence is racist and tied to colonial histories of racialisation, Orientalism and Othering; it fails to account for the way that contexts produce violence, for example, contexts of poverty, austerity, structural racism, Islamophobia, foreign policy, border violence etc create conditions of violence and legitimate grievances that disenfranchise people when there are no avenues to express them or freely protest, critique or dissent.

By not addressing this and instead concentrating on Muslims and ideology, Prevent problematically puts the onus on individual Muslims for any and all violence. Subsequently, expressions of 'Muslimness' become suspicious in of themselves and it is being Muslim that is assumed to be the precursor and cause of violence. Hence, Prevent has bolstered an atmosphere where having a beard, wearing hijab, speaking Arabic, praying in public, etc. have all become securitised issues – things that make you seem more suspicious/potentially criminal (think of See It, Say It, Sorted). In this way, Prevent is nothing but state-sanctioned policing of Muslims based on pre-emptively assuming we're all on the verge of engaging in acts of political violence.

For more on this read,
Arun Kundnani, *The Muslims Are Coming*, 2014.
Arun Kundnani, 'Radicalisation: The Journey of a Concept', online article, 2012.
Derek Silva, 'Radicalisation: The Journey of a Concept Revisited', online article, 2018.

BRITISH VALUES

Young Muslims In Britain Often Straddle Two Worlds / They Appear to Have
a Foot in Each Culture / Concerns Revealed Around the National Identification
of Muslims In Britain / Review Raises Alarm Over Social Integration in The
UK / Schools to Promote Fundamental British Values / The Face Of Britain Is
Changing Beyond Recognition

I look in the mirror
it's not shattered, I am whole
no one foot in, one foot out
no reason I've got to learn Britishness from the somehow more devout

I'm not 'uneasy' 'torn' or 'straddling'
it's not shattered, I am whole
yet the opposite is somehow all that you'll get told

I mean I guess cos if it wasn't
if we faced up to the glass
you'd be left with the fact that I am inside
I am Britain now, cos

Britain is bismillah
Britain is basmati rice
Britain is box braids and black barbers' shops, Bollywood and bhangra
Britain is Bradford and Barking and Birmingham
Britain is biriyani and black beans
Britain is black, Britain is brown
Britain is boys blasting dubstep on the bus to town
Britain is body-popping outside the tube
Britain is Brick Lane before it was cool
Britain is bilingual
Britain is the burka
Britain is praying in the changing rooms

Britain has its feet in your sink
Britain is bad at knowing itself, belligerent, and boring.

Britain has not *Changed Beyond Recognition*
recognise it was never one thing

I am the inside you pretend is outside
but we have to stop pretending

Pretending the rolling hills are just romantic
not remnants of injustices swept under a rug
like the tea didn't come from Asia
like its sugar wasn't grown by slaves
like dry humour isn't a way to just ridicule dissent
and queues don't expose the way we're always told to wait for change
rather than making it

and it's funny that over-apologising is seen as a national trait
cos half of history is still waiting

I look in the mirror
it's not shattered, I am whole
there is no 'brink' or 'turning point'
I'm here.

Britain is barbaric
- oh sorry, did you think that was me?
Barbaric bystander straddling the boundary?
Not quite inside so you could say I'm the things you forgot
like you're 'modern' so I'm 'backwards'
you're 'democratic' so you say I'm not

when the truth is
Britain is blood on its hands and back-to-the-wall
Britain is selling weapons to the most repressive regimes in the world

Britain is the bombs the Saudis drop on Yemen
Britain is using fear to build surveillance apparatus since 9/11

Britain is believing in human rights whilst removing them all
Britain is Yarl's Wood, Brook House, Colnbrook and Morton Hall
Britain is sixteen hundred dead in or after police custody since 1990
Britain is no qualms about detaining asylum seekers indefinitely

Britain is suicide attempts, secret courts and secret torture
Britain is stopping you at the border
Britain is Seeing it, Saying it, Sorting it - which means
Britain is also deporting it

cos what else do you do
when you look in the mirror and find

the sugar and tea had strings attached
the factories on the rolling hills depended on our labour
the bombs destroyed the homes of kids now at the border

Britain is barbaric
Britain is blindly patriotic
Britain is built on false narratives
slices of other people's dishes

Britain is stolen artefacts in museums named after itself
Britain is knife and fork polite, stabbing you at will
Britain is selective:
yours 'til its not; in yours 'til its not, then blaming you

Britain is borders
Britain is Brexit
Britain is spending on weddings but not fire-proofing homes
Britain is cutting mental health services yet somehow 'Strong & Stable'

Britain is 40% of young people in custody being from ethnic minority
backgrounds
Britain is blaming them for this statistic, rather than asking difficult
questions

'cos
Britain is blaming the kids who aren't white
Britain is blaming the Muslims
Britain is blaming the immigrants
Britain is blaming bureaucracy

Britain is not listening
Britain is Not That Great
Britain is breaking
but breaking everywhere except the place it points the finger

because there's only a few things left that are Great about Britain
and they're that

Britain is bismillah, basmati and bilingual
box braids and black barber's shops
Bollywood and bhangra
body-popping outside the tube
Brick Lane before it was cool
Britain is the burka
Britain is praying in the changing rooms
Britain has its feet in your sink
Britain is your greatest nightmare
every repercussion you never thought through

Britain is the terror to be countered

Britain is the mind to be got inside

I am the Great in Great Britain now
and aren't you terrified?

'British Values' are a set of four values introduced as part of the government's Counter Terrorism strategy, particularly in schools. Promoting British values is therefore something that education providers are expected to do under the Prevent Duty which became a legal duty on public service providers in 2015. The Duty connects teaching 'British Values' to 'preventing' young people being 'drawn into terrorism'. British values are defined as democracy, rule of law, individual liberty, and mutual respect and tolerance of different religions. To me this is very ironic since Britain has been one of the most violent and undemocratic nation-states in the world's history through its role in the trans-Atlantic slave trade, colonisation and imperialism, and direct and indirect involvement in wars and genocides. Through this poem I wanted to convey those ironies and show that the narrative Britain tries to promote to define its 'values' or 'itself' is really a project to define racial Others (people of colour and Muslims) as 'outsiders' to Britain. It is a way to deflect from and to not have to deal with the violence that the government and state create and perpetuate. It is a way to say 'we are not what they are, and what they are is whatever we say we are not'.

By defining Britain as democratic and tolerant, undemocratic tendencies and intolerance are displaced and scapegoated onto 'out-siders'. Subsequently 'Britishness' becomes a glorified imagining which in the end translates to nothing more than whiteness. I say this because the 'promotion of British values' relies on an assumption that they need to be taught to children from ethnic minority backgrounds (who are more associated with extremism and violence through measures like Prevent and structural racism), whereas government reports (e.g. The Casey Review, 2016) assume white children/areas with less 'ethnic minorities', are more likely to have 'British values' already. Since the whole concept is so clearly racialised (seen as something white people are born with and 'ethnic minorities' need to learn, develop and prove), and since no inherent or static 'British culture' has ever existed (Britain has never been geographically, ethnically, physically or ideologically one thing, cultures/nations never are), this poem tried to reveal the ironies of the charade and highlight that what Britain says it is contradicts what is actually does.

Further information on specific lines of the poem:

Britain is the bombs the Saudis drop on Yemen refers to the way BAE systems, a British company that supplies arms, technology, planes and training to Saudi Arabia is central to making Saudi Arabia's war in Yemen possible. UK arms exports are leading to the murder of civilians in Yemen which many have argued is a deliberate strategy – targeting civilians is illegal under International Law. Where is Britain's 'rule of law' at play here?

Britain is sixteen hundred dead in or after police custody since 1990 – since 1990 Inquest report that 1712 people have died in police custody or following contact with the police (June, 2019). 14% of those deaths were of BAME people, but BAME deaths occurred disproportionately due to use of force and restraint, showing the palpable racial dimensions of police violence.

Whilst we associate police violence with the USA and Black Lives Matter movement there, institutional racism in the UK police force also kills, 1712 is not an insignificant number. Is this the rule of law? Is this mutual respect?

Yarl's Wood, Brook House, Colnbrook and Morton Hall are four of eleven immigration detention/removal centres in the UK. Such centres are places where people who are seeking asylum (over 50%), 'undocumented' (without visas or paperwork mostly due to being refugees, trafficked or having experienced other violent conditions), and otherwise waiting to find out if the Home Office will grant them 'leave to remain' or deport them, are held. People can be held in these centres indefinitely – this means there is no maximum time limit on people's time in detention in the UK – it could be months or years – the UK is unique within Western Europe for this.

In 2017, over 27,000 people were held in immigration removal centres across the UK. Since 2000, at least 39 people have died in UK detention centres (according to Inquest). Not only are detention centres effectively cages to hold and punish the most marginalised in, indefinite detention causes unbearable mental health problems due to the uncertainty and stress and there have been many reports of the physically and sexually abusive conditions in detention centres, too. Article 9 of the Universal Declaration of Human Rights says no one should be subject to "arbitrary arrest, detention or exile", these centres clearly violate the principle of basic human rights... Which British Value does this align with? Or are those values not afforded to you if the Home Office believe you don't have the right to be in the UK/don't have the right paperwork?

For further information follow the work/social medias of:
SOAS Detainee Support, End Deportations and Detention Action

Britain is secret courts and secret torture refers to the fact that the 2013 Justice and Security Act introduced 'closed material procedures' meaning that the government can decide a case without giving any details or evidence to the defendant. All or part of a claim can be heard in closed proceedings that exclude even the claimant who is represented by a 'Special Advocate' who is not able to speak to the client once they have seen the 'sensitive material' of the case. Is this 'the rule of law' that is a central 'British Value'?

For further information, read:

Nisha Kapoor, *Deport, Deprive, Extradite: Twenty-first Century State Extremism*, 2018.

Britain is deporting it refers to the expulsion of people from the UK based on asylum claims being refused, visa/claims expired, or the Home Office deciding you are a danger to "the public good". The 'Windrush scandal' in 2018 when people (particularly British people from Caribbean countries who arrived in the UK before 1973) were detained, denied legal rights, threatened with deportation and deported (83 people) by the Home Office was a case of deportation that did not fit these already awful categories. Other deportation and extradition cases as well as removal of citizenship have also affected others through Counter Terror legislation – see more at dde.org.uk.

THIS IS NOT A HUMANISING POEM

Some poems force you to write them
the way sirens force their way through window panes in the night
and you can't shut out the news, even when you try

write a humanising poem
my pen and paper goad me
show them how wrong their preconceptions are

be relatable

Write something upbeat for a change, crack a smile
tell them how you also cry at the end of Toy Story 3
and you're just as capable of bantering about the weather in the post
office queue
like everyone, you have no idea how to make the perfect amount of
pasta, still

feed them stories of stoic humour
make a reference to childhood
tell an anecdote about being frugal
mention the X factor

be domestic
successful
add layers

tell them you know brown boys who cry
about the sides of Asads, Amirs and Hassans they don't know
the complex inner worlds of Sumaiyyahs and Ayeshas
tell them comedies as well as tragedies

how full of life we are
how full of love

but no

I put my pen down
I will not let that poem force me to write it
because it is not the poem I want to write
it is the poem I have been reduced to

reduced to proving my life is human, because it is relatable
valuable, because it is recognisable
but good GCSEs, family, and childhood memories are not the only
things that count as a life
living is

So this will not be a 'Muslims are like us' poem
I refuse to be respectable.

Instead
love us when we're lazy
love us when we're poor
love us in our back-to-backs, council estates, depressed, unwashed
and weeping
love us high as kites, unemployed, joy-riding, time-wasting, failing
at school
love us filthy, without the right colour passports, without the right
sounding English
love us silent, unapologizing, shopping in Poundland
skiving off school, homeless, unsure, sometimes violent
love us when we aren't athletes, when we don't bake cakes
when we don't offer our homes, or free taxi rides after the event
when we're wretched, suicidal, naked and contributing nothing

love us then

Because if you need me to prove my humanity
I'm not the one that's not human

My mother texts me too after BBC news alerts
'are you safe? Let me know you're home okay?'
and she means safe from the incident, yes
but also safe from the after-affects

so sometimes I wonder
which days of the week might I count as liberal?
and which moments of forehead to the ground am I conservative?

I wonder
when you buy bombs is there a clear difference between
the deadly ones that kill
and the heroic ones that scatter democracy?

Isn't it really 'guilty, until proven innocent'?
How can we kill in the name of saving lives?
How can we illegally detain in the name of maintaining the law?

I can't write it.

I put my pen away.

I can't
I won't write it

Is this radical?
Am I radical?

Because there is nowhere else left to exist now.

I wrote *This is not a humanising poem* a few days after the "London Bridge Attack" on 3 June 2017. I was living in London at the time and as it was Ramadan I had been at Regents Park Mosque on that night. As I came out of the mosque I saw a text from my mother asking if I had seen the news and to be safe going home. I experienced the sinking feeling so many of us know – I knew something bad had happened involving a Muslim person perpetrating violence and I knew that that made me, a visibly identifiable Muslim woman, unsafe. I tried to write a poem about that feeling: the complication of wanting to distance myself from the attackers to show I didn't deserve any backlash personally, that Muslims shouldn't all be painted with the same brush – however, in trying to write that poem I realised that I was falling into a trap. The trap was that in trying to prove I was not deserving of violence or stereotypes because I was relatable /familiar to non-Muslim mainstream society, I was accepting the premise that my humanity was conditional upon my being relatable in the first place. My humanity is not something to be earned, it is a virtue of my being alive. When a white man perpetrates violence, we do not assume that all white men are worthy of backlash and potentially mass-shooters unless they prove otherwise. In other words, their humanity is not conditional upon them "proving" anything, it is a given.

Moreover, in trying to distance myself from the attackers to show I didn't deserve backlash, I was implicitly buying into the 'Good Muslim' category. The Good Muslim is only ever a status that can be achieved by condemning Muslims who perpetrate violence, and in so doing, distancing oneself from the 'Bad Muslim'. However, in this project of proving Goodness to attain respectability and individuality, we invest in the idea that there are some Muslims (Bad) who do deserve treating with suspicion and violence - the ones who do not vocally 'prove their humanity' and therefore may be 'Bad'. This is very problematic as it means that the act of trying to position oneself as a Good Muslim actually reinforces the narrative about Muslims as inherently 'Bad' by default, and therefore as violence as something pathological and essential in Muslims rather than an outcome of specific contexts and circumstances. Because I realised this, I wrote this poem instead of the other one. I reject the premise that my humanity is conditional; I reject that premise because it dehumanises me.

I refuse to prove my humanity. I am not interested in deserving or earning my God-given right to humanity, in fact I am more interested in asking why it is conditional in the first place. What is made possible by my humanity being premised on me fulfilling certain conditions? What is able to happen if I am assumed to be guilty/suspicious until I prove otherwise? Well, if I am dehumanised or seen as inherently suspicious/related to criminality and violence, then inhumane treatment of me (/Muslims/people of colour) is justified. This includes indefinite detention, deportation, occupation, imprisonment without trial, use of secret courts, social death via gentrification, murderous negligence like Grenfell, the list goes on.

Dehumanising people was essential for the projects of colonialism and slavery, therefore our ideas of "humanity" are deeply linked to race. Whilst much formal colonial occupation is over, this controlling and deciding the value of lives based on how "human" they are deemed to be continues with violent consequences.

This poem gained 2 million views online.

For further information, read:
Arun Kundnani, *The Muslims Are Coming*, 2014.
Nisha Kapoor, *Deport, Deprive, Extradite: Twenty-first Century State Extremism*, 2018.

ACKNOWLEDGEMENTS

It is completely surreal that this collection exists. Ten-year-old Suhaiymah always wanted to be an author but there's no way she ever thought she'd be a poet. I have been blessed beyond belief with the opportunities I have been given through people, places and moments that are the trajectory that made this collection possible. All the praise, the thanks and the glory is for Allah, but I also want to extend my gratitude to as many people as I can who made this possible directly or indirectly.

I want to thank Mairi who pushed me to go to my first open-mic night and perform; Charlotte Higgins for making that a night I felt welcomed to and excited by; the Cambridge UniSlam team of 2016 for picking me to be part of it and experience my first big slam; all the student societies and groups who programmed me for garden parties and events throughout 2015-2016; Robin Lamboll for telling me that I had to apply to the Roundhouse Poetry Slam in 2017 since I was living in Camden; Daria and Kristen for coming out to support me in the first heat of that slam and backing me all the way, always (and for everything else I can never put into words, thank you); Bava, Hiya, Sumaira and Sabiha for being the real troopers and day one fans (and Bava especially for trying to be my agent and merch-maker despite all anti-capitalist tendencies).

I want to thank all the poets, activists, and people I have met since that first heat in 2017; Helen and Colin David for their generous and open-ended support; the Khidr Collective for being one of the first platforms to ask me to perform in London and for being consistently supportive and having my back; every platform, event, student, poet and persistent emailer who has since asked me to perform. To Amerah Saleh who gave me a multitude of big opportunities the first time I ever met her; the ILL LIST Slam who invited me to California to perform internationally for the first time; every poet and welcome heart I met during my month in the USA.

I have to thank Asim Qureshi for being one of the very first people to extend me generous and genuine support and see the essence of my work, for commissioning me my first commission and for always,

always, pulling me up. I will never be able to thank you enough. For the @MuslimAcademics (you know who you are) who I learn everything from and then co-opt into my poetry – keep up the hard grafting; for Aisha Mirza for your heart and constant duas; for all the scholars, writers, authors and academics who I have learnt so much from - particularly those who are people of colour.

To Lola Olufemi, Waithera Sebatindira and Odelia Younge for embarking on my first publishing journey with me; to FLY; to Mariam Ansar for being who you were to me at that time; to all the young women starting or at University who have ever messaged me or asked me for advice.

I have to thank everybody I met in Pakistan during my three months there in 2018. A special and unreserved thanks to Allajaway who will never be able to read this collection but who undoubtedly made me a better writer and is a better poet than most poets I'll ever know. Also, to Nazia.

I want to thank everybody who supported my patreon account for the year I had it and showed me such kind support and love; to all my teachers who ever bolstered me in the way that made me believe I could dream to be an author; to Mr Carmichael for your love and boundless enthusiasm; Mr Bennett for being the first teacher to make writing the most exciting thing in the world; Mr Pearce for making me believe I was capable of changing the world; and Miss Jay for being my Miss Honey and making me believe I was Matilda.

I want to thank everybody who has invited me to their University, city, protest or poetry night to perform (or tried relentlessly), or everyone who has been consistently supportive of my work since day, or everyone who has advised, connected or platformed me at any point, or who I simply draw inspiration and faith from or has impacted me at some point (even if you don't know it) – I can't name all of you but special thanks to Mohamed Mohamed, Sabrina Mahfouz, The Repeat Beat Poet, Hana Jafar, Sofia Rehman, Hanain Brohi, the Just Rhyme team, Sheetal and Shirin, Shoomi and Dulon, Theatre Uncut, Shahina, The Yoniverse, Kamil Mahmood, Freedom Studios, Sailesh, Lighthouse Books, all the iSocs, all the femsocs and women's officers, HHUGS,

Heaux Noire, everyone at Devil's Dyke Network, Undleeb, the Round-house, Imam Shakeel and Imam Ashraf at Lewisham Islamic Centre, Shaheen Kasmani, Sabeena Akhtar, Zain Dada, The Muslim Vibe, Hamja Ahsan, Nisha Kapoor, James Trafford, Suhraiya Jivraj, Iqra Choudhry, Azeezat Johnson, Alaa Alsaraji (for making the cover happen!), Qasim, Tasmia and Raeesa, and Lowkey for asking me to perform at his London album launch in 2019 as well as the endless continued support, advice, experience and being the example par excellence - and everyone else I've surely missed!

I owe a huge and love-filled thanks to the 'Clash of Civilisations' group chat - to Phelan, Abdulla and Jess for being the only three people who might remotely understand this collection's name; thanks to Phelan for all the enabling and brilliant politics; thanks to Grace Phillip for believing I was a poet before anybody else had hardly even heard my poems, for recording them, uploading them, making whole documentaries with them – your love is the kind I want to emulate; to Ellen, Emily, Megan and Vicky for your love; and to Faye Guy for giving me the boost of institutional legitimacy that an 'English student' would actually write about my poems.

Thank you to Stuart at Verve Poetry who made this happen, for putting up with me never emailing back and unsurprisingly seeking extensions. Thank you for supporting me so keenly and making me believe this collection should exist.

Finally, I couldn't have got here without Saffana and Jamal, thank you for being there when I'm at my tiredest and most frazzled, for backing me so much – Saffana, thank you for all the voicenotes, the love, the advice and outrage at me not backing myself – thank you for not only believing in, but creating the hype; Jamal, thank you for being one of the two people I trusted with the penultimate draft of this manuscript, I took all of your advice, and thank you for making my transliterations make sense. I also could not have got here without Amina Jama. Amina, you're an angel. Thank you for helping me fight the imposter syn-drome, for reminding me that poetry looks a million different ways, for always giving me time and knowing exactly what to say, for telling me to put myself first, to put my vacation responder on, thank you for being wise beyond your years. Thank you for taking all the time out to read my work so generously and thank you for being proud of me – you have no idea how much I love and am proud of you.

The gratitude that I can't really express in words goes to my Nani and Nana. I will never be able to thank them for even the smallest of the things they've done. Nothing, none of this would be possible without them and this can never be a thank you for the heartbreaks and traumas they've they've endured so that a kid like me could have the luxury of writing poems about us all. May Allah grant them the highest ranks in Jannah.

To Saifur Rehmaan and Sumaiyyah, you two are my heart, thank you for being who you are, thank you for keeping me grounded, thank you for forcing me to freestyle and being better off-the-cuff poets than I'll ever be after weeks of rehearsals – I love you forever.

And last, but only because the immensity of the thanks I owe you is impossible to comprehend, thank you Mummy. Any good in me is from your cultivation and your belief in me. Thank you for giving me wings and telling me to fly, for giving me armour, faith and courage. All I can say is that I pray Allah gives you the best of both lives, grants you jannah without reckoning, showers you in light and love and laughter, and that I am by your side there. Being loved by you has been one of the greatest honours of my life and really, if this collection is a dedication to anything, it is a dedication to you, my role model, my jaan, my captain, my king.

سُبْحَانَ اللّٰهِ وَبِحَمْدِهِ عَدَدَ خَلْقِهِ وَرِضَا نَفْسِهِ وَزِنَةَ عَرْشِهِ وَمِدَادَ كَلِمَاتِهِ

ABOUT VERVE POETRY PRESS

Verve Poetry Press is a young press focussing initially on
meeting a local need in Birmingham - a need for the vibrant
poetry scene here in Brum to find a way to present itself to the
poetry world via publication. Co-founded by Stuart
Bartholomew and Amerah Saleh, it is publishing poets from all
corners of the city - poets that represent the city's varied and
energetic qualities and will communicate its many
poetic stories.

Added to this is a colourful pamphlet series featuring poets who
have previously performed at our sister festival - a poetry show
series which captures the magic of longer poetry performance
pieces by poets such as Polarbear, Matt Abbott and Second City
Poets. But most importantly we are open to publishing anything
that we feel demands to be in print, anyone whose words we
feel need to be heard. In January 2019 we published *A Fly Girl's
Guide to University* edited by Odelia Younge for this reason and
now bring you *Postcolonial Banter* by one of 'Fly Girl's' co-
authors - the incredible Suhaiymah Manzoor-Khan.

Like the festival, we strive to think about poetry in inclusive
ways and embrace the multiplicity of approaches towards this
glorious art.

www.vervepoetrypress.com
@VervePoetryPres
mail@vervepoetrypress.com